HEAL the WAY JESUS HEALED

Scientific Healing
from
The Quimby Manuscripts

Written
through the character of

Richard Dale Lode

Truth Center Books
213 second Street
Box 424
Sioux Rapids, Iowa 50585

Info@TruthCenterBooks.com

Copyright© 2018

All rights reserved. No part of this book may be reproduced in any form without written permission from Truth Center *Publishing.*

ISBN-13:978-1983928789 - ISBN-10:198392878X
Title ID 8013237

Table of Content

My Theory
The Healing Principle
The Errors of World
Two Sciences
Christ and Truth
True And False Christs
My Religion
Happiness
Prayer
More About Prayer
What Do People Really Believe?
Harmony
Resurrection
My Use of the Word Mind
The Natural Man
The Scientific Man
Death of the Natural Man (1&2)
How The Senses Are Deceived
The Senses and Language
Man's Identity
Imagination
Mind and Disease
The Relation of Truth to Sickness
Cures
A New Theory for Cures
Disease
What Do I Impart To My Patients?
Mind and Disease
God and Man
The Christian's God
Jesus and Truth
Love
Jesus' Healing and His Mission
Religion
The Effect of Religion on Health
What is Religion?
The Other World
No Religious Put Downs

FOREWORD

THE HEALING PRINCIPLE

It is an undisputed fact that Quimby cured disease without any medicine or outward applications. How did he do it is the question that agitates and interests people. If he had any new way different from the mysterious and superstitious mode acknowledged by others, what is it? Where did he get his power?

He denied that he had any power or gift superior to other men, but he contended that he operated intelligently under the direction of a Principle which was always his guide while with the sick. He followed this Principle in practice and theory, and under it he learned facts of real life that he could never get in any other way.

He found the way by which all errors can be corrected.

It might be called the Principle of Goodness. It is the highest intelligence that operates in the affairs of man, always producing harmony, and making man feel that he has more to learn and is a progressive being. It was always Quimby's aim to develop this principle in relation to human misery and make life a science. He said, "The cause of all man's misery is in ignorance of himself, and in proportion as he develops this higher, happier life science, he sees through all his misery, and in proportion as he sees through them he can correct them." With a knowledge that all trouble and disease is a false alarm he proceeds to undermine their foundation, and the structures give way. He says, "No matter how well-established are the facts of any disease, their basis is all wrong, dependent on the false opinions of men for their existence and therefore curable through a change of belief.*"*

Quimby identifies the patient's belief associated with his illness, changes the patient's mind about the belief, this change of mind destroys the illness, and that is the cure.

MY THEORY

All effects produced on the human frame are the result of a chemical change within the human body, and all the varieties and changes are accompanied by a particular state of mind. When your mind has been deceived by a false belief you put this belief into the form of a disease *without your knowledge*. By my theory or truth I come in contact with your enemy, the false belief, and restore you to your health and happiness.

This I do by talking with you until I discover the false belief and correct it. This establishes the Truth, and the Truth is the cure. I use no medicine of any kind, nor am I affiliated with any religious practice or medical profession. I am only guided by the dictations of my own conscience.

A sick man is like a criminal cast into prison for disobeying a law. Like a lawyer I plead his case, and if I get the verdict the criminal is set free. If I fail, I lose the case. The persons own judgment is his judge, his feelings are his evidence. If my explanation is satisfactory to the judge [the person himself], he will give me the verdict. This ends the trial, and the patient is released from his illness.

THE ERRORS OF WORLD

What is your position in regard to the world and the errors of the world?

If you embrace the world you embrace its errors and become a servant to its laws, and thereby the spirit or truth departs to the God that gave it. But if you hold on to the Truth the world is in subjection to you, and instead of becoming a servant you become a teacher of Truth to the world, to lead other minds to the Truth.

Instead of your happiness being dependent upon the world, your happiness is dependent upon the Self within you. Here is your true position, and this is the struggle you will have to go through, "Shall the world lead you, or shall you lead the world?" This is the point that is to be settled in your mind.

Now I will give you the signs of the times. Many shall come in the name of the Truth, and say, do this, or do that, but Truth says beware, be not deceived, *seek first the truth, and all will be pleasure and health to you*. Then you can take the lead, and the world will listen to you. Then the kingdom of this world has become subject to the Kingdom of Heaven, or error has become subject of Truth. This is a trying scene to go through, for to the Satan of your senses, so to speak, it will seem as though you must leave all the world's pleasure, and seclude yourself from society. But this is not the case at all; you will like society all the better. You will rejoice with those that rejoice and weep with those that weep, and your happiness will be their happiness. Then will the old ideas or errors of the world come and knock at your door for admittance, but you will say, "Depart from me, for when I was hungry and naked you gave me no food or clothing, when I wanted truth you gave no answer."

TWO SCIENCES

There are two sciences, one of this world, and the other of a spiritual world, or two effects produced upon the mind or matter by two directions. The wisdom of this world acts in this way: It puts its own construction on all sensations produced in the mind, and establishes its knowledge after the effect is produced. For instance, a child feels a pain in its head, the child has no idea what it is, and if the mother is as ignorant of its origin as the child, no effect at any moment is produced. But the wisdom of the world arrives in the form of a lady. She hears the account of the pain from the mother, and assuming a wise look, gives her opinion in regard to the trouble, and says the child is threatened with edema [swelling] of the brain, because she saw the same symptoms of another child who died of that disease. This account excites the mother, whose mind acts upon the child. The explanation of the supposedly wise lady gives direction to the mind and presently the work commences to show that she is right. A doctor is called who is as wise as the lady, and not being willing to be outdone by her he puts in a few extras like congestion of the brain, says the lady was right but did not get the whole of the matter. So he has two chances after the child dies to prove his superior wisdom over the lady.

It sometimes happens that a controversy arises between the two parties, each trying to establish their own opinion so as to have the disease turn their way. In the meantime the patient is left to her own self and gets well. This is the only good result I ever saw from such a controversy. The patient is a mere tool in the hands of these blind guides who attempt to cure her. While this controversy is going on, seeing that all each party wants is to establish their own way, the mother sends for me in her dilemma. I arrive and a fire-brand is thrown in between the combatants. I contend that the child has no edema of the brain, but only some slight shock upon its mind, and quieting the child is all that is necessary for a cure. Here the controversy ends. If the mother employs me I prove my theory and the child gets well. If they prove theirs they kill the child, and an examination is made which establishes their theory, and I am a humbug or quack. If I take the case, the child gets well, for the child was not sick, only a little nervous.

CHRIST AND TRUTH

This is the thing we must decide, whether there is a knowledge or truth independent of man, or whether truth is the offspring of an organized religion. *Jesus said truth was independent of man and called it the Son of God. Peter called it Christ. The people confused the personal Jesus with the Christ and in ignorance confounded the two together, and called it Jesus Christ. This last construction has given rise to all the religious wars and bloodshed since the Christian era.*

Now let us look at the controversy. This makes two worlds, ignorance the one, and Truth or Science the other. These two powers act upon every man. One is identified only with the body, the other is identified with truth or science. Jesus gave some of the traits of that power identified with only the body when He said, "it is of the earthly man," and when He said, "Out of the heart proceedeth all kinds of evil thoughts." These thoughts are like mental matter, and are the result of error, superstition and ignorance, without any knowledge of God.

Science is the opponent of the above, and as it accounts for all phenomena, ignorance is destroyed. Science has had to fight this battle with the world of error and ignorance before it could establish its standard and take its position above the natural man. Then it is acknowledged and worshipped in spirit and in truth. Before it becomes a science it is under the law of ignorance and superstition, directed by blind guides leading the blind, through the knowledge of this world, and this wisdom Jesus calls foolishness with God. Now to separate these two, so that the wisdom of this world shall become subject to the knowledge of God, is not an easy task.

As it has never been explained how Jesus did His healings the people have looked upon them as miracles. But to suppose Jesus performed a miracle is to suppose Him ignorant of the power He exercised, and if so He was just as much a quack as those He condemned; for He said, when accused of curing through ignorance or Beelzebub, "If I cast out devils through Beelzebub, my theory or kingdom cannot stand, but if I do it by Science, it is not of this world, but of God, and it will stand." Here He makes a difference between ignorance and knowledge. Again, if Jesus was ignorant of His power, and did not know how to explain it to others, why did He tell His disciples to go out in all the world and heal all manner of disease? If He could give no explanation of His manner of curing, He was as ignorant as they. But I am certain that He knew more than His disciples could understand, and as soon as Jesus was crucified, the cures ceased to be done by a Science, but went back into the hands of priests and magicians, and have seemed to be miracles ever since, and the Christ that prompted Jesus' acts is not known at all. The Christ's method of healing never did any doctoring, nor offered up prayers, nor creeds. It never belonged to this world, nor talked about any kind of religion. It talked itself. Itself was its life, and its life was the healing of the sick and distressed. It takes the feelings of the sick and knows their wants, and restores to them what the world has robbed them of. This is the Christ that was crucified many years ago. Now the only thing we hear is what was said about Him. Yet He is in the world but has no identity as a Science.

TRUE AND FALSE CHRISTS

I will try to explain the true Christ from the false Christ, and show that "Christ" never was intended to be applied to Jesus as a man, but to a Truth superior to the natural man — and this Truth is what prophets foretold. It has been called by various names, but is the same truth. There is a natural body of flesh and blood — this was Jesus. *His mind like all others was subject to a law of truth that could be developed through the natural man.* This power Jesus tried to convince people of, as I am trying to convince people that there is such a state as intuition, that is, that there is a power that has an identity and can act upon the natural man, which the natural man is ignorant of. When this power acts upon his senses it acts in the form of an idea or thought. *The natural man receives it like the servant, but acts as though he was the father of the idea.* The world gives him credit for this superiority over the rest of his fellow men.

But unwilling to admit this power, the world attributes it to some unknown cause. People would rather have it be a miracle rather than a science, for otherwise it would lower them in the estimation of themselves and cause their own destruction, as all truth destroys error. *This belief, that there is an intelligence independent of ourselves, has always been admitted*, but attributed to some miraculous power from another world.

TRUE RELIGION--IS GOODNESS

I lay claim to no religious faith independent of my acts. When I have faith in my religion, I talk it and put it into practice. When I am not putting my religion into practice, then if I talk it I am talking about nothing real. This is a distinction that may at first seem curious to some, but if you will look at it rightly you will see there is more in it than you would at first suppose. One of Christ's followers made a remark like this in regard to the same distinction. He said, "religious faith independent of works is only idle talk. I will show you my religious faith is real through the heart felt works I perform. *There is no such identity as goodness by itself.*"

HAPPINESS

What is happiness? It is what follows any act of the law of science, but it is not always understood. Man is the medium of two laws; the one, chance or ignorance, which is of this world; the other, God or Science, which is of a higher world. The wisdom of one is called the law, the knowledge of the other is called the Gospel. These two laws enter into all our acts. The introduction of the one, the Gospel, is the destruction of the other to all those who understand. To introduce a Science that can explain the errors that keep us in trouble is what prophets foretold and wise men have looked for ever since the world began. This knowledge has been called by various names. It was called the New Jerusalem that came down from heaven, and it was called the Kingdom of Heaven. This is the law written in the heart; it is the knowledge of ourselves.

It may be asked, how can we distinguish between the two, for everyone has a right to his own opinion? That is true, but science does not leave it answered in that way, but proves it so that there can be no mistake. Now as disease is an error, so the mind, as in any error, must be corrected by a power independent of itself, and this power must be governed by a science in all cases; though it may not be necessarily understood by the person applying this power. As Science, God acts like a balance which judges correctly. It contains no [mere] thought or reason, but judges everyone according to his worth. The Christ Science to the natural world is looked upon as mystery, witchcraft, sorcery, etc., because the natural world cannot see anything beyond itself. But there is a Mind that can teach it, and another that can learn it. Then comes the end of the world of error, and the introduction of a more excellent Gospel of God. All religions that embrace creeds are of this world, governed by laws which contain rewards and punishments. To hold out inducements to be good with one hand, and punishments with the other, is not the religion of

Christ. He is in us, and a part of us, and to know ourselves is to know Christ, and the result of this knowledge is Goodness and the effects of goodness is happiness.

To be a follower of Christ is not so easy a matter as some might think. It is easier to talk about religion than to walk it. To walk it is to put it into practice, and to put it into practice is to give everyone that asks of you some spiritual food or knowledge, that will cool their feverish tongue, or soothe their excited brain, and lead them like the true shepherd to their home or health, where they can rejoice with their friends. *To be a follower of Christ is not an easy thing, but to be a representative of the world is not very hard, it only requires one to become as ignorant as a child.*

To call yourself a follower of Jesus, is to call yourself a pattern of goodness. This is our happiness and the happiness of others, for we are all workers for the same truth. Therefore dismiss error, and embrace the true Christ Science, and fight the enemy of health, like a soldier of Science.

PRAYER

Can any good come out of prayer? I answer yes, but not in the sense that is supposed. A phenomenon can be produced in the same way that is brought about by hypnotism, but there is no knowledge in the church-prayer. It is the effect of superstition and ignorance. It is not of Christ, but from a mind ignorant of self and God. Man often prays because he wants a favor to be rewarded to him for more than he deserves.

True prayer is the desire of the heart, and *if the heart is right the prayer will be answered.* For as the heart is only the figure or emblem of knowledge, a true heart must have scientific knowledge, and a corrupt heart must be full of superstition and ignorance, deceit and hypocrisy.

One great argument offered in favor of prayer is that Christ said, "He who humbles himself shall be exalted." And what the narrow minded believe is required of a person to humble himself is to get down on his knees and ask for God something which he is not entitled to. But God rewards everyone according to his acts, and He knows our wants before we ask. So to ask of a Being whom we acknowledge knows our wants is either to curry favor or flatter Him with the idea that we think He will be pleased to see how much we honor Him. This is the wisdom of this world, but not the wisdom of God. God asks no such worship. To worship God is to worship Him in spirit and in truth, for He is in the truth, not in the error. Our reward is in how we think and act and if we think and act rightly and honestly we get the reward. If we act selfishly we get the result also. *He who expects God to leave Science and come down to ignorance and change a principle for a selfish motive to please Him, is either a knave or fool and knows not God.* God is like the fire which throws heat or love on all around. Those who will can enjoy the heat or love, but if we choose to stand out in the cold, we cannot expect exclusive privileges; for God has no respect to one over another. I have no account with God, He pays me as soon as my work is done, and I do not ask favors of Him apart from His principles. If I think and act wrongly He will not step out and correct me. I must do it myself. If I think and act rightly I get my reward, for our happiness or misery is in how we think and act, and as we are a part of each other, our happiness is in our neighbor also, and *to love our neighbor as ourselves is more than all burnt offerings and sacrifices*. If you understand this, Jesus said, you are not far from the Kingdom of Heaven. Jesus had no sympathy with the hypocrites' prayers. He warned His disciples and the multitude against all such prayer. His prayer was that God would forgive them for they knew not what they did. *A desire to know God, is a desire to know ourselves*, and that requires all our thoughts to come into that happy state of mind that will lead man in the way to health. This is a science and is Christ's prayer.

ABOUT CHURCH PRAYER

I look on church-prayers as I do on all other errors that have been invented to govern mankind and keep the people in ignorance of themselves and God. You may ask if I would destroy prayer. No, but I would put into man a higher law that would teach him to worship God as a God of science and knowledge. This law would put to death the law of ignorance. For prayer is the law of man, not of God, and makes God nothing but a mere sorcerer or magician to frighten the ignorant and superstitious.

Why should the explanation of Christ's mission which was to heal the sick, destroy death, and bring life and immortality to light, be left to persons who have no sympathy for the sick, but who by their interpretation of Christ keep man sick and ignorant of himself? Of what advantage has Christ been to the sick, according to the common opinions of mankind? *Does the priest relieve them of any burdens? If not, where is the benefit of the church-prayer?* It is in contradiction to Christ's own teaching. What was Christ's idea of church prayer? He called it hypocrisy and a blind guide to lead the blind. He warned the people against those who prayed in the streets, told them to obey all the laws, but not to believe in the doctrines, for they laid burdens on the people grievous to be borne. *Now, if these burdens were their belief, Jesus must explain them away in order to relieve the people of them; And his explanation was their cure.* Therefore He said to them, "Come unto me all ye that are weary and heavy burden, and I will give you rest." Jesus's explanation was his religion, but their religion contained all the superstition of Egyptian darkness, prayers, sacrifices, and burnt offerings.

Jesus did not condemn any of the above, but He had a knowledge of the errors man is subject to and His mission was to bring science to light in regard to our ignorance or darkness and to put man into a state where he might, by relieving the sufferings of his fellow men, be of some advantage to himself and to the world. His religion was not of this world, and the world knows Him not. Christ is God or Science, and to know God is to know Science and put it into practice so that the world can be benefited by it.

Once Jesus was asked by a scribe, "What is the first commandment of all?" Jesus answered "The first commandment is Hear, Oh, Israel, the Lord our God is one Lord." Here He admits a supreme power, and says, "Thou shalt love the Lord thy God with all thy heart, and thy neighbor as thyself."

The young man said unto Him, "Well, Master, thou hast said truly, for there is one God, and there is none other than He, and to love Him with all thy heart and soul is more than all burnt offerings and sacrifices." Jesus saw that he had answered discreetly and He said unto him, "Thou art not far from the kingdom of God." These questions and answers were given before the whole multitude, and I see no reason for disputing Jesus' own words by putting a misconstruction on some passage, and making Jesus something that neither He nor anyone else ever thought of. He was accused of making Himself equal with God, but that was their ignorance, which gave that construction, and if I had not been accused of the same thing a hundred times, I might put the same construction on Jesus as others do. But I can see, and show to the sick beyond a doubt, the difference between Jesus and Christ, and the difference between the two words gives a very different meaning to religion. *The church's construction makes our acts and lives one thing and our religion another. Jesus made our acts the effect of our knowledge and in proportion as we understand Science we understand God, and acknowledge Him in truth.* This Science separates us from this world of error and death and brings life and immortality to light, and this Science was what Jesus taught. Ignorance of Christ or Christ Science put "Jesus" and "Christ" together and said "Jesus Christ." For superstition could not account for any of the cures that Jesus made except they were from heaven, and although Jesus tried all in His power to convince them to the contrary, He could not. The religious people of Jesus day, like the Christians of today, made heaven and hell places independent of man, and although some may deny it, their acts give the lie to their protests.

Most people pray to a being independent of themselves, acknowledging a state or place where God is, and when they pray, supposing that He listens, ask Him to hear their prayers and relieve their wants. This is precisely what the heathen did, and Jesus called them hypocrites and condemned them, for He said this offering up of prayer and sacrifices year after year could never take away sin or error, so Jesus embraced Christ or Truth and laid down His own life for the happiness of mankind. Before this the world knew not Christ or Truth. This truth Jesus taught, and His teaching was the healing of the nations, and if His truth had not been misconstrued, the world at this time would have been rid of thousands of errors it now has. This was Jesus' truth, which to the people was a mystery and seemed to embrace only a belief, for a truth to a person who cannot understand it is a belief. But Jesus labored to convince the people that it was a science, that the fruits of it were seen in His practice, and that it could be taught.

WHAT DO PEOPLE REALLY BELIEVE?

To some this may seem a strange question, but it involves more than we think it does. Our belief includes all the errors in our religious opinions. Our opinions which contain errors are the foundation of all our misery, while our happiness is in the true knowledge that follows the correction of the errors in our opinions.

To illustrate, *when we have a problem it is because we have an error in our opinion and are in trouble about it*. But when the answer comes and the error is corrected our happiness accompanies it. Then there is no more ignorance or sorrow. Error and ignorance have passed away, all has become new, and we are as we have been. We have all the happiness we want; the misery is gone, and the spirit is ready to solve another problem.

Now the problem I wish to solve is what I first named. Do we really believe in what we think we do?

I answer, "No," and shall show that we deny what we profess to believe in almost all we say and do, thereby proving ourselves either hypocritical or ignorant. We profess to believe in Christ, that He is God, that He knows all things, and is capable of hearing and answering our prayers. We also believe that man is a free agent, that he is capable of judging between right and wrong, and believe that if man does not do right he will be punished.

When asked for proof of all this, we are referred to the Bible.

When we ask an explanation of how Christ cured, we are told it was by miracle.

If we ask if Christ knew all things, the answer is, "Yes."

Then if we ask, did He know what He was about, what He did, and how He did it? The answer again is "Yes."

Then if you ask how He knew, they will answer, "It is a miracle," or "The ways of God are past finding out," — and thus you are left in the dark.

Now those who reason this way will not accept any fact not based on their faulty reasoning. The fact is they aren't reasoning at all, and are accepting what they have not the slightest proof of, except for the explanation of some person of doubtful existence.

Now, when I show that I can produce a phenomenon that to all appearance is just like some produced by Jesus, I would like to know by what authority anyone dares to say that it is not done in the same way that Jesus did His works. If they cannot tell how I do it, or how He did it, how do they know that it is not done in the same way? Their only objection can be that it happens to be contrary to their own opinion, which is not worth anything, and they admit it; for they will say it is a miracle to them. This makes them what Jesus said of such guides. He called them blind guides leading the blind, and warned the people against them. He called them whited sepulchers, and all kinds of names, and the world has been led by such guides ever since.

HARMONY

Can two persons be in harmony except they be agreed? If you are affected by any person in a way that produces fear, you cannot be in perfect harmony with another till the fear is cast out. If it is from some idea that affects your character, you will be imprisoned in the idea till free from it. The idea may or may not be accompanied by an individual, but if it is so accompanied you will be affected by that person in your sleep, the same as in your waking state. One of these effects is attributed to the natural mind, and the other to the spiritual mind, but both have the same effect on health.

To separate us from what we look upon as truth is not a very easy task, for sometimes we think we like the very thing we really hate. This keeps us in ignorance of ourselves. When we would do good evil is present with us. It is not ourselves but the evil that dwelleth in us. This evil comes from the knowledge of this world, and as this world is made up of flesh and blood, no true knowledge is in it. To separate us from the error, and bring us into harmony is to explain the false idea away, and then all sorrow will pass away, nothing will remain save the recollection of what is past, like a dream or nightmare, and you will not be likely to get into the same error again.

All sensation, when first made, contains no direction, but is simply a shock. Error puts a false construction or opinion upon it, and speaks disease into existence. The mind is then imprisoned in the idea, and all the evils that follow are what we call disease. I shall speak of two kinds of disease. One is called by the doctors, local, the other nervous. I make no difference as far as the effect of the mind is concerned. Nervous diseases are the effect of one's opinion reduced to a belief, and so are all others. I will state two cases to show the difference. A person is exposed to cold weather. Ignorance and superstition, have reduced this sensation to a process resulting in a person getting a cold because he believes cold weather causes colds. This is set down as a real disease, and so it is, but it is based upon an ignorant superstitious idea. This is one of the errors of this world, but judged by this world as a proven fact because of the effect cold weather seems to have on the body. This is called "real, and no mistake."

Now, tell a person that there is a serpent in his breast, or that there is a hell that will torment him in case he does not act or believe just so, and when you have succeeded in making the person believe this, seeing him tormented and miserable you turn about and accuse him of being fidgety or nervous. This is the result of accepting the world of opinion as Truth.

To condemn all this folly is to disbelieve in all peoples' opinions that tend to make one sick or unhappy. Let God or Truth be true, and all men liars. If two ideas come in conflict in you, investigate the wrong and you will find that it is someone's opinion that you have tried to carry out, to your own destruction. You have mistaken some opinion for a truth. This makes all the trouble.

RESURRECTION

It has been generally taught that there is a resurrection of this flesh and blood, or that this body should rise from the dead. This absurdity arises from the fact that man began to philosophize before he understood himself. Man is superstitious from ignorance. He sees through a medium of ignorance called his five senses, therefore he sees nothing outside of his belief. *His reason is a part of his belief, therefore he is to himself just what he thinks he is*, and his belief tells him that his life is in his body and when his body dies, he dies. Therefore when he speaks of life he speaks of saving it or losing it, as though it were something independent of or separate from himself. Therefore we are taught to believe that Jesus came to make all things right, suffered and died and rose again, to let us know that we should rise and live again. We are told that man had wandered away from God, and had become so wicked that it was necessary that something should be done, or he would be in danger of being banished from God's presence. What was required of him in order to be saved was to repent and return to God, therefore his life depended on him believing that he should repent or he would be damned.

Now, what are we told to believe today? In the first place, we are told to believe that Jesus, the man, was Christ or God, and that he died on the cross to pay a penalty for our sin. We are told that if we do not believe it, we must be damned. Now you see that our lives are in our belief, and our belief is made up of someone's opinion who knows just as little as we do.

I, for one, do not reason in that way. I know that man has two identities, one in this state called the physical with its disease and death, and one in the spiritual or scientific state. Death and life are the two identities. Life is the Spiritual Knowledge of our eternal existence, which has no matter. Death is the name of that state of mind that reasons as the natural man reasons. The life of

MIND

The natural man, whose intellect is linked with the brutes, and who cannot see beyond matter, reasons this way: Although he is in all matter [everything] he believes he is outside of it observing it. He cannot see his absurd mode of reasoning, but it is shown in disease. He thinks he is composed of fluids and flesh, and also mind. He believes his mind to be the offspring of his body and brain, therefore he can only believe in a superior wisdom as a mystery. The fact that he admits to it as a mysterious gift or power shows that he does not know it. To make man know himself is to convince him, that he, his wisdom, is above the world and distinct from his belief. Then his mind will be given an identity embracing everything that has a beginning and ending, but sickness and disease will have no part of it. I developed this identity, with its accompanying wisdom, which is the real man, until I broke through the illusion of beginnings and ends and could see beyond the world of opinions into the light of Science. I can now see that things have being, and how we take our opinions for truth.

The moon is a figure of the natural man. Its light is borrowed from the light of the opinions of the sun. It thinks it has light of itself, but the sun light knows that it is the reflection of the sun's light. *The wise man in like manner knows that the light of the body or natural man is but the reflection of the scientific man.* If the natural man lacks this knowledge of himself he walks in darkness and stubbles at every turn. This is the prison that holds the natural man, till the light of Wisdom bursts his bonds, and sets the captive free.

Who makes the Scientific man?

The first cause or God.

How?

By attaching Science to the identity called the natural man.

Then does Science have an identity?

Yes.

What is it?

The Wisdom or God.

What is it like?

The Scientific man is not of flesh and blood, but of that world where error never comes.

How do we know of it?

It speaks through the Scientific man.

What does?

The life or the wisdom of God.

Where and how does it differ from the natural man?

In everything. The natural man is only an idea The Man of Science uses for the development and evolution of Himself.

MY USE OF THE WORD MIND

I will now try to explain what man is, and what he is not; and show that what he seems to be, he is not, and what he does not seem to be, he is. I will illustrate the two men so that each shall be a separate and distinct identity. I will take for my illustration the natural man as we see him, and the man of Science who cannot be seen, and show how they differ.

The natural man is made of flesh and blood.

The man of Science is not.

Man has life. *Science is life.*

Man has sight. *Science is sight.*

Man has feelings. *Science is feeling.*

Man has all of the five senses.

Science is all of the five senses.

Man of himself cannot do anything.

Science can do all things.

The natural man is of matter.

The man of Science is of spiritual substance.

Then what is the natural man?

Nothing but the scientific man's faulty idea of life and death.

this state depends on faulty reasoning, for it can only reason through what it can experience through its five senses. It reasons that life is part of it, but at the same time acknowledges that life is something that can be lost or saved. Death also reasons with the idea that it can save its life, yet invents all sorts of diseases which destroy its state of self. It fasts and prays and observes forms and ceremonies, all in an attempt to save itself. It is very strict in its laws to protect its life. Its opinions it calls Knowledge and Truth. It fears God or Science. The destroying of its opinions it calls death. These beliefs are from the knowledge of this world, and are the inventions of man; but the wisdom of this world is foolishness to God or Science.

The wisdom of God, or real Life, does not go into the clouds to call truth down, nor into the deep to call God up, but shows us that *God is in us, even in our speech*. It sees matter as a cloud or substance that has a sort of life (in the appearance). It sees it move around. It also sees commotion, like persons moving to and fro upon the earth. God's wisdom is not a part of this world, but it can come into it and reason with its followers who are imprisoned by their belief. *To be free from this world is to know that an opinion is not knowledge, and when this is found out the opinion is destroyed and Science or Truth takes its place.*

THE NATURAL MAN

All mankind have respect for wisdom or something superior to themselves that they cannot understand. Man of himself is naturally indolent, brutish, and willfully stupid, content to live like the brute. He is pleased at any trinkets and trifling things. He likes to imitation and tries to copy whatever pleases him; in this he shows reverence for his superiors. As he does not possess Science he is often deceived. Thus he is made timid and willing to be led. His courage is the courage of ignorance and when he sees superior numbers he curls down like a dog when whipped by his master. Easily led and easily deceived, no confidence is to be placed on his word, for his word is always like the wag of a dog's tail, to show his submission. But when his ends are answered, his next act might be to injure the one that had saved him from trouble.

Now because the brutes can be taught something it does not follow that they can be taught Science. They have their bounds which they cannot pass. So the natural man has his bounds which he cannot pass. But when I speak of the natural man, I speak of that wisdom that is based on an opinion. *The brute is undergoing a change by the introduction of the wisdom of man and becoming the natural man. So the natural man is undergoing a change by the introduction of the Scientific Man.* The brute is developed as far as the wisdom of man is capable of instructing him. So Science takes the natural man of opinions and instructs him in the Wisdom of God. As every man has more of the wisdom of opinions than of Science, he is ignorant of himself, and being ignorant he can see only one character; for all the wisdom he has is public opinion. He is up today and down to-morrow, and knows not what is the cause of his rise or fall.

THE SCIENTIFIC MAN

I will try to define what I mean by the scientific man or man outside of matter. To do this I must assume myself in relation to mind as God stands to all creation. *The natural man is only an idea made by God's wisdom, like a shadow.*

After this shadow goes through a certain change like any other matter it is in a state to be a medium of a higher power than itself. God sent an identity of His wisdom to take control of the medium and carry out His design and bring man to a knowledge of the Father. This identity that He sends is Science or the Son of God.

To illustrate I must use a figure so you can get my meaning. For if you do not do the thing God does you cannot be the Son of God. Jesus was called the Son of God. Why was He called the Son of God? Because He did the will of His Father who sent Him. To be a Son of God you must do His will, and His will is to subject your errors to the Truth, so that you can know that you are born of God. Now, I will suppose that God, when He spoke man into existence, knew that man was His own idea. An evolutionary change was going on for a certain time till man became of age, or men became ready to be governed by a higher principle than matter. Science is this principle put into practice. So Science is the Son of God or Wisdom. Now Science being the Son of Wisdom, it is a part of Wisdom. Give this Science an identity with a knowledge of its Father and then you have a Son ready to take possession of matter when matter becomes purified, or an evolutionary change has taken place in it so that it can be governed by an independent power. . . . This Son or Science is not seen by the natural man, so the natural man thinks his life is in this belief. Now to come to the knowledge of this Science is the new birth.

DEATH OF THE NATURAL MAN (I)

The senses of the natural man are attached to his knowledge, and that is made of opinions, and so his senses are attached to his opinions. His opinions embrace all belief. So to destroy his belief is to destroy his life, for his life is in his belief, and a part of it.

I will show you where I differ from Christians and in fact all other sects. If you will admit that mind is spiritual matter, for the sake of listening to my ideas, I will give you my theory. I assert that according to man's beliefs there are certain falsities and also some facts established beyond a doubt. I also assert that as my wisdom is not of this world, or man's belief, it follows that what I know I have no opinion about, it is truth only. *All knowledge that is of man is based on opinions. This I call this world of matter; it embraces all that comes within the so-called senses.* Man's happiness is in the truth and his misery is in his opinions that are not true, in other words is in his beliefs that are in error, but the wisdom of science is of God's complete truth, not of man.

I will separate the two worlds of which I am now speaking. The world of opinions is the old world. That of Science is the new, and a separation must take place and a battle fought between them. The world of error and opinions has held Science in bondage ever since man began to be independent of savage life. The child of Science has been nourished in the bosom of its mother in the wilderness of error until it grew up so as to assume a character, then whenever it undertook to assume its rights it was always met with the thunder of error from the world of matter. But the enemies or error could never completely prevent its growth, for its growth was in the scientific world, and that world has no matter in it. So the scientific man can pass through the errors and instruct the child of Science till it bursts forth. Then the natural man or error falls down and worships the scientific laws and acknowledges them as king of his world. Its kingdom is of Truth, not of error; therefore it is not of this world of matter. Its habitation is in the hearts of men. His house is not made with hands but is in the scientific world. So his whole aim is the happiness of man. *The scientific man sees through matter which is error acknowledged as truth, although it is to the natural man a reality.* As error holds on to all territory under its power it tries to keep the scientific man in slavery or bondage. To keep the Science of Life down the natural man invents all sorts of humbugs in the shape of invisible things and attributes life to them. It is almost impossible to tell the scientific man from the natural man as both communicate through the same organs. As the scientific man has to prove his wisdom through the same body as that of the natural man he is often misrepresented and put down by false stories of the errors of the natural man. *This was where Jesus found so much trouble in His day, for the people could not tell who was speaking, the personal Jesus or the Universal Christ.*

To be in the scientific world is to acknowledge a wisdom above the natural man. In that world wisdom sees through matter. This is the condition of those who enter into the intuitive state. To them matter is only an idea that may or may not be seen. But when this explanation is given to blind guides who have eyes but cannot see, ears but cannot hear, and hearts that cannot understand, they become afraid, lest this truth destroys their current belief system. The death of error, to them, seems to be death of themselves, but in reality is the introduction to the Science of Life and Happiness.

I will now try to explain this Science and upon this solid rock you can build your Life. Thoughts, like grains of sand, are held together by their own likeness or attraction. The natural man is composed of these particles of thought combined and arranged to make a form called man. As thought is always changing, so man's mind is always throwing off particles or thoughts and receiving others. This change of mind is under one of two directions, either of this world of opinions, or of God or Science, and *his happiness or misery is the result of his thought.* The natural man has always been under the wisdom of this world, the scientific man has always been kept down by it. *No man except Jesus has ever risen to that state where the scientific man could control the wisdom of the natural man.* This has always caused man to be at war with himself. *In this warfare if the natural man rules, disease and unhappiness are the fate of man. If Science rules, health and happiness are his reward.*

Now, like Jesus, I stand alone on this rock, fighting the errors of this world, and establishing the Science of Life by my works. What is my mode of warfare? With the axe of truth, I strike at the root of every tree of error and hew it down, so that there shall not be one error in man showing itself in the form of disease. *My knowledge is my wisdom and is not matter or opinion.* It decomposes the thoughts, changes the combinations and produces an idea clear from the error that makes a person unhappy or diseased. You see I have something to reason about, and this something is eternal life, which is in the Science Jesus tried to establish.

If I can show that man's happiness is in his correct belief, and his misery is the effect of his beliefs in error, then I shall have done what never has been done before. Establish this and man rises to a higher state of wisdom not of this world, but of that world of Science which sees that all human misery can be corrected by this principle. Then the Science of Life will take its place with other sciences.

I will show the world's reasoning and how I reason differently. I will talk of the oracles of the world, for all science of this world of opinions has oracles. These oracles of which I speak are those who pretend to instruct the people in regard to health and happiness. The first is the clergy, for they take the lead in everything pertaining to man's happiness. When I ask them what they think of Jesus, His mission, if He had any, and of what advantage it was to the world, here is what they say:

"The world had gone so far astray that it was necessary to send Jesus Christ into the world to convince man of a future state of rewards and punishments, so that he might repent and be saved."

When I ask, "Have you any proof of this or is this only an opinion?" They respond:

"The Bible."

When I ask:

"Does the Bible speak for itself or does someone explain it? They answer by saying,

"We must take the Bible as our guide to truth."

Let us now sum up the wisdom which this oracle has delivered:

All of his wisdom is founded on an opinion that there is another world and that Jesus came from that world to communicate the fact to the inhabitants of this one. *The happiness of man is not increased by this theory, because this oracle cannot cure the sick.* Now Jesus cured the sick and said if they understood Him they might do the same. We want a theory like that of Jesus, not of talk, for a theory that cannot be put into practice is worthless.

My oracle is Jesus: He proves the goodness of wisdom. *Jesus was the oracle and Christ the wisdom* shown through this man for the happiness of the sick. Who has not been deceived by the other two classes, the priests and doctors. God or Wisdom has seen how these blind guides have robbed the widow and the poor of their treasures, leaving them despairing and dependent upon the charity of a this world.

This wisdom of God developed itself through the man Jesus and He fearlessly stood up and denounced these blind guides as hypocrites and devils.

DEATH OF THE NATURAL MAN II

I will give some experiments of a man of wisdom [the scientific man] acting through and dissolving the man of matter [the natural man] so the man of wisdom, the scientific man, can escape. This process is Christ Science. Take for example two persons, or you and myself. One wishes to communicate to the other. You feel a pain, I also feel it. Now the sympathy of our minds are mingling together, but there is no wisdom in it, for wisdom is outside of matter. If we both feel the same pain, we each call it our own; for we are devoid of that wisdom which would make us know we were affecting each other. Each one has his own identity and wants sympathy, and *the ignorance of each of us affecting the other is the vacuum that is between u*s, yet we are drawn together by this invisible action called wanting sympathy. Now *make a man wise enough to know that he can feel the pains of another, and that wisdom will get him outside of matter. The wisdom that knows this has eternal life, for life is in the knowledge of this wisdom.* This the world is unacquainted with.

Now Jesus had more of this life or truth than any other person, and to teach it to another is a science. If you know it and can teach it, you are a teacher of the truth. But if you know it and cannot teach it, you are a follower of the truth. Now *the knowledge of this truth is life, and the absence of it is death.* There are a great many kinds of life. The natural man begins at his birth. Animal life is not vegetable, and vegetable is not animal life. And there is another kind of life that is not understood, and that is the life that follows the knowledge of this great truth. Jesus, was acknowledging His possession of this Life when He said, I (Christ) and my Father are one."

I shall show that Jesus was not life, but life or Christ was in Him, and He taught it. He says: "Whosoever will save his life shall lose it, and whosoever shall lose his life for my sake shall find it." The people believed their life to be in themselves. But *Jesus knew their lives were in God, for if they lost their opinions and found this Truth, then they had lost their life and found it.*

I will now take a rose for an illustration. You are like a rose. You throw from yourself an atmosphere or vapor. When the rose is a seed all outside of it is darkness to the germ of the bud. This is you as the child. As the rose opens it expands and unfolds itself to the world, the same as a child's brain expands and opens the folds of its understanding. As the rose comes before the world of roses it takes its stand with the rest of its kind. So it is with man. As he unfolds his knowledge, he is classed with others of his kind. As the rose throws off its peculiarities to the air, the world judges of its odor. So as man throws off his peculiar character of health or disease, the world is judge of his happiness or misery by the fruits of his belief.

Take a person with a disease. The idea of disease decomposes and throws off an odor that contains all the ideas of the person affected. This is true of every idea or thought. Now I come in contact with this odor thrown from you, and being well I have found by experience that these odors affect me, and also that they contain the identity of the patient whom this odor surrounds. This called my attention to it, and I found that it was as easy to tell the feelings or thoughts of a person sick as to detect the odor of spirits from that of tobacco. I at first thought I inhaled it, but at last found that my spiritual senses could be affected by it when my body was at a distance of many miles from the patient. This led to a new discovery, and *I found my [real] senses were not in my body, but that my body was in my senses, and my knowledge located my senses according to my wisdom.* If a man's knowledge is in matter all there is of him (to him) is contained in matter. But *if a man's knowledge is in Wisdom instead of matter then his senses, and everything else about him, are outside of matter. He is like a man standing beside himself that is watching himself.* He *is watching not only what he does, but more importantly, he is watching his thoughts and his motivations*. To know himself as the man witnessing himself is the truth of who he really is, and the effect is life in this truth, and this truth is in Wisdom. So *the man who knows all this is in Wisdom with all his senses and life*.

You may ask if all I say is true what is it good for? If it is only a belief, I admit that it is of no more value to a person than any religious belief. You may ask for proof that will give some light upon the subject. I will give it, as near as a man who has eyesight can explain colors to a blind person. When I sit by a patient, if he thinks he has disease of the heart, the atmosphere surrounding him is his belief, and the fear of death is in the density of the clouds of his mind. Now knowing he is in the clouds somewhere I, as it were, try to arouse him. But it appears as though he were blind. So I shake him to arouse him out of his lethargy. At last I see him aroused and look around, but soon sink back again. By my talk I disturb the clouds, and this sometimes makes the patient very nervous, like a person coming out of a fit or awakened from a sound sleep. What I say is truth, and being solid it breaks in pieces his matter or belief, till at last he looks up to inquire what has been the trouble. My explanation rouses him and gives another change to his mind, and that is like a thunder storm. When it thunders and the lightning flashes, the patient is nervous. When the cloud of ignorance passes over and the light of truth comes, *then the patient sees where his misery came from*, and that *it was believing a lie that made him sick*. My arguments are based upon my knowledge of his feelings, and this knowledge put in practice is the Science of Health and is for the benefit of the sick and suffering.

HOW THE SENSES ARE DECEIVED

Why is it that I run a greater risk of being misrepresented in regard to my mode of curing than practitioners of other schools? I must be allowed to offer my own explanation of this fact; because if I were understood I should not be in danger of being misrepresented and condemned by the guilty. I stand alone, a target at which all classes aim their poisonous darts, for I make war with every creed, profession, and idea that contains false reasoning. Every man's hand therefore is against me, and I am against every man's opinion.

Man's senses may be compared to a young virgin who has never been deceived by the world. Popular errors are like a young prince who stands ready to bestow his addresses upon all whom he can deceive. When he approaches the virgin he appears like an angel of light and wisdom. By soft speech and imposing address he wins the virgin maid to his belief. Having become entangled in his web or false doctrines, she is carried away from her home or state of innocence into the gulf of despair, there to live a miserable existence. In this state a false theory holds out to her all kinds of ideas and she becomes a slave to the world. Wisdom is banished and error like a raging lion goes about devouring all whom it can find.

The above was written from the impressions that came upon me while sitting by a young lady who was afraid of dying, and also was afraid of being blind. It may seem strange to those in health how our belief affects us. *The fact is there is nothing of us [the natural man] but belief.* It is the whole capital stock in trade of man. It is all that can be changed, and embraces everything man has made or ever will make. Wisdom is the scientific man, who can destroy the works of the natural man. **Disease is made by the natural man's belief in some false idea.** The error comes to the virgin mind and makes an impression. The soil is disturbed and the mind listens or waits to be taught. If it is misled, briars and thorns and troubles spring up in its path through life. These all go to make the man of belief. Wisdom destroys these false ideas, purifies the soil, and brings the mind under a higher state of cultivation. This is the work of Science. When a person has made himself a body of error and death, truth destroys his death, and attaches his senses to a body of life.

THE SENSES AND LANGUAGE

Why is it that mankind have settled down on the fact that man has five senses, no more, no less? The wise say the spiritual man has two more, making seven. Now, what is a sense? If "senses" mean what the wise say it does, why is man set down above the brute? Let us see how they compare. Man sees, hears, tastes, smells and feels, and so does the brute. When you ask where is man's superiority you are told that man can gain wisdom through being able to reasons and the brute cannot.

Now all will admit that there is a vast difference between a wise man and a brute, but *this wisdom that makes man above the brute is not of this brutal world, but comes from a higher source.*

Now all will admit that God is superior to man in regard to wisdom, and if we can show that *man's senses can act independently of his natural body*, if it can be shown that man's wisdom is not of matter but of God, *we will divide him into as many senses as it is necessary for the making of the scientific man.*

The savage is a fair specimen of the natural man and the wild beast is a fair specimen of the brute creation. One has no preeminence over the other — "might is right" — each is happy when not disturbed. But disturbance brings other senses into action, and *as wisdom is developed it gives man a knowledge of himself above the natural man of five senses. Thus the wisdom of the scientific man sees the man with the five senses, a little above the brute, in error trying to free himself from his earthly matter*, or ignorance, and arrive at knowledge of phenomena that keep him in a state of error, disease and death. So I will leave the man of five senses in error and talk to the scientific man about the other senses.

The scientific man is not embraced in one idea. He may be scientific in many areas of science such as mathematics, chemistry, astronomy, All this is acknowledged and admitted by even the natural man, though not understood. But the Science of Christ or Happiness is not acknowledged by the wisdom of the five senses. It requires more senses to put men in possession of the Science that will teach them life, peace, and happiness.

As happiness is what follows a belief it is necessary to know whether our wisdom is of this world of opinion or of the world of Truth or Science.

The world of the natural man sees nothing outside of its senses.

The wisdom of the scientific man sees nothing in the natural man's senses but ignorance, for the wisdom of this world is opposed to the Science of Happiness or Christ.

MAN'S IDENTITY

We often speak of man's identity as though there were but one identity attributed to him. This is not the case. Man has as many identities as he has opinions, and the one his senses are attached to last is the one that governs him. This may seem strange but it is true. *Our senses are not our identity*, because they cannot change, *they are principles*. But our belief, thoughts and opinions can change. So when we say a person never changes it is as much as to say he is only a brute. We say that our tastes change. Does the principle change, or our belief? The fact that we are aware of the change shows the change must be in that which can change.

Then what is it that does not change? It is that Principle that never moves, the foundation of all things. It is that which says when we have found out something new, "Why did you not find it out before?" It says to us when we are investigating certain mathematical truths, "This truth has always existed." This something is Wisdom. It does not come or go, but is like light. You cannot keep it out of sight, in fact you acknowledge it in every act. But *that which acknowledges it is not the something acknowledged*. It witnesses the something acknowledged. For instance, if you work out a problem aright, you acknowledge a wisdom that existed before you knew it. *Our need is to get our senses attached to this Wisdom.*

IMAGINATION

This power of forming ideas called imagination is one of the highest elements in the human mind, and it is the foundation of all true discovery. Yet like all scientific facts it is abused and misrepresented.

To give you a clearer idea of the misuse of this word I will illustrate it by a religious belief. Church members never use the word imagination in speaking of their belief and their religion. Do they mean to say that they believe without also creating the image of their belief? The fact is that religious beliefs are founded in deception and the leaders deceive the people into them. At the same time outsiders are skeptical and apply the words "imagination" and "superstition" in derision. *Every person wishing to deceive the masses calls everything imagination that does not coincide with his belief.* The medical faculty have assumed to themselves the power of creating by imagination every idea based on wisdom. All ideas opposed to them are said to be false, and they say that the imagination that creates these ideas is a disgrace, and belongs to ignorance and superstition.

A physician, for instance, may tell you the most absurd falsehood that his imagination can invent, but it is "true" because *it has the sanction of the faculty*. If you believe him you use the power which if rightly applied is one of the best of faculties for the purpose of *creating a disease* which you have taken for a truth. There is no dispute or controversy about that. But if some outsider should deceive you half as much and you should create an idea you would be accused of being superstitious, believing everything and imagining all sorts of humbugs.

The word imagination is so misapplied that it has lost all the value it ever had, and like religion it has a name without meaning covering numerous deceptions applied to weak-minded people. I never use the word as others do. When people think they have a disease which I know they have not, I do not ascribe it to their imagination, but to *the fact that they have been deceived.* A physician may tell you what is not true about yourself. If you believe it and he deceives you that is no disgrace to you, for it shows an honest heart and confidence in the physician. Then follows the creation and appearance of the thing he has told you. As far as you are concerned you are blameless, but the physician is a liar and hypocrite and has used your creative powers to deceive you for his own selfish ends. Now when their hypocrisy and deceit are exposed they cry out, "humbug, our craft is in danger: this quack works upon the imagination of the sick and makes them believe the medical faculty are not honest."

Let me call your attention to one fact; the word *imagination never applies to the first cause. There is a superior power that originates, and imagination does the work and produces.* Christ Science detects the direction that is given to imagination and corrects it if false. All men have gone out of the way, and no one reasons from Science, so Wisdom saves them all by introducing the light of a new mode of reasoning that will separate error from truth. This includes the subject of health and happiness.

No one knows the mischief or the misery that physicians of all kinds make by their opinions, and this never will be known till man learns that his belief makes his trouble.

I know that a belief in any disease will create a chemical change in the mind, and that a person will create a phenomenon corresponding to the symptoms. This creation is named disease. The doctor can produce a chemical change by his talk. It makes no difference what he says. A phenomenon will follow to which he can give a name to suit his convenience.

For instance, a person gets into an excited, heated state and a doctor is called. He gives medicine which affects the patient and he feels better. That then is what the patient needed and the doctor has the credit. If the patient grows worse and the medicine makes him sick; the doctor says he has the symptoms of a fever, while in reality he himself has been the cause of nine-tenths of the trouble.

Men must be given then the knowledge of one great truth, that he must be aware of and choose between two different principles: wisdom which is seen in Science, and error which is seen in matter or in opinions. The latter is governed by no principle known to man, but is simply the action of cause and effect; but man who sees only the phenomenon puts wisdom into it, for the cause, the believe in an opinion, is never seen. To the natural man this is a mystery.

The spiritual senses are all that there is of a man. Therefore when he changes his senses it is necessary to know what he gains or losses by the change and also what he embraces. To suppose a man has but five or even seven senses is as absurd as to suppose he has but a certain number of ideas. His senses are himself, what he knows and what he thinks he knows. Paul divides man into two identities: Wisdom or what could be proved by a science, and knowledge or what man believes to be true. So when a man says he thinks he knows or believes he knows it is sure that he does not know as he should. The scientific man sees and knows himself, and he also sees and knows his opponent, but the man of opinion can only see the scientific man in a mystery. As Wisdom advances in man the effect is to destroy the senses [belief] which are attached to knowledge. When knowledge overbalances a man's wisdom, his error reigns, but if wisdom is in the ascendency his knowledge becomes subject to his wisdom. In mathematics, chemistry and all the arts and sciences that can be demonstrated, knowledge submits to wisdom, but that part of man's senses attached to knowledge that is not subject to science is religion, disease, and politics. These are false sciences based on opinions. They are the same that Jesus denounced as false prophets, evil and blind guides who deceived the people. These errors embrace that part of man that believes in sickness, death, and all kinds of superstition. They beget tyranny and selfishness in man and slavery in nations. It is the mission of true Science to destroy these, and Christ Science will be developed till they are destroyed.

Therefore where man's confidence in these opinions is at an end his senses will seem to be annihilated, but in reality he will be like the young eagle which has burst its shell and soars aloft on the wings of wisdom, where he looks down upon the earth and sees the natural man crawling like a reptile waiting to devour the child of science as soon as it is born. Todays Wisdom is the child of God. It is now breaking its shell and assuming its freedom; and its enemies, like those of Christ, stand ready to devour it as soon as it is born.

I wish to make you understand these two characters, Science and opinions. Give to each an identity like a man and separate one from the other, and then see which you follow; for you must follow one, you cannot serve both at the same time. If you serve Science, you are in your wisdom and know it. If you serve opinion, you have no wisdom but your life is in a belief that can be destroyed, so you will live all your life subject to bondage through fear of death. But *if you have passed through death or opinion to the life of Science, death will have no power over you.* Disease is death and the belief in death causes fear, therefore if death is destroyed the fear is gone. *It becomes us then to search into the causes of the phenomenon called disease and find if it is not an image of our own making.* The Jewish people were making all sorts of false beliefs that tormented them. So God through Moses says, "Thou shalt make no graven images" to represent any false idea which they had been taught, nor worship any superstition, for truth was jealous of error. It always condemns our error and rewards our scientific acts. *Disease was conceived in priest-craft and brought forth in the iniquity of the medical faculty.* The priest prophesied falsely and the doctors flourished by their lies, and the people swallow it up as if they love it.

Then the question arises, what can you do to prevent it?

I say, let your mind be like a sponge, absorb the Christ Science that will wash away your errors and diseases with Truth.

Come out from the world of opinion, and when a doctor says you have so and so, make him prove it.

MIND AND DISEASE

I have often spoken of the word mind as something which I call spiritual matter. I use this term from the fact that man cannot conceive of wisdom except as attached to matter. We always speak of mind as different from matter, one is visible and the other is invisible. There is another element called reason which sees the effect, but is ignorant of the cause. We are all taught to believe that mind is wisdom and here is the trouble, for if mind is wisdom then Wisdom cannot be relied on, for all will admit that the mind changes. Jesus separates the two by calling one the wisdom of this world and the other the wisdom of God. If we understand what He meant by "this world" we can follow Him.

I have spoken of that element in man called reason. This is a low intellect a little above the brute which is the link between God and mind, and the same that is called by Jesus the wisdom of the world, for this world is another name for spiritual matter. Now mind is the spiritual earth which receives the seed of Wisdom, and also the seeds of the wisdom of this world of reason. Disease is the fruit of the latter, and the application of the wisdom of God or Science is the clearing away the foul rubbish that springs up in the soil or mind. This rubbish is the false ideas sown in the mind by blind guides, who cry peace when there is no peace. Their wisdom is of this world that must come to an end when the fire of Truth runs through this world of error.

THE RELATION OF TRUTH TO SICKNESS

What course of argument must be used to make the masses understand this truth by which I correct the errors that make man sick? What relation has this truth to the sick? It is the sick man's friend. Let me explain through the use of a parable.

A lady came to visit me saying that her physician had examined her lungs and found the left one very infected. This she believed and when I told her that her disease was in her mind, it was as much as to say she imagined what was not the case. I told her she did not understand what I meant by the word mind. Then taking up a glass of water I said, suppose you should be told that this water contained a poisonous substance that works in the system and sometimes produces lung problems. If you really believe it, every time you drink the tea the idea of poison would enter your mind. Presently you begin to hack and cough a little. Would your fears then grow less that the water was poison? I think not.

Finally you are given over by your doctor or friends and call on me.

I sit down by you and tell you that you are nervous and have been deceived by your doctor and friends.

You ask how?

You have been told what is false, that the water you drink contains a slow poison, and now your cure hangs on the testimony in the case. If I show that there is no poison in the water then the water did not poison you.

What did?

It was the doctor's opinion put in the water by your mind. As the mind can receive an impression so it can also be changed by an impression. By calling the water pure, which is the truth, it is easy to show that the mind can be changed by a wisdom superior to an opinion. This wisdom that acts upon the mind is something that never has been described by language, but it is looked upon as a superior "power." This power gives rise to all religious opinions. Man has tried to condense it into a being called God, and he worships it. My theory is based on this something that man is ignorant of and develops from it a language as comprehensible as any language. I call it the Christ science or the science of life or the science of happiness. It contains no words but speaks from impressions which cannot be mistaken if man knows himself.

CURES

I am often asked what I call my cures. I answer, the effect of a Science. *Science is Wisdom put into practice.* To the natural man it is a power or mystery. All wisdom that has not been acknowledged by the natural man is called a "gift" or spiritual demonstration, not a science. The curing of disease has never been acknowledged to be under any wisdom superior to the medical faculty, so people have kept the world in darkness till now, and how much longer they will do so I cannot tell. If I succeed in changing the minds of men enough to investigate they will see that disease is what follows an opinion [a mistaken belief], and that wisdom or Truth will destroy the opinion and make the cure. Then the cure will be attributed to a superior Wisdom, not a power.

I am accused of interfering with the religion of my patients. This is not the case, but if a particular passage in the Bible or some religious belief affects the patient I attack it. For instance, a person gets nervous from his belief that he has committed the unpardonable sin. His thought is attached to a passage in the Bible that he believes applies to his case. I know this is all false, so of course I have to destroy his belief [opinion], and this destroys the effect which is the disease. His senses are attached to a belief [opinion] that is causing the disease, mine are attached to the Wisdom that shows the absurdity of the opinion. His wisdom is of man, mine is of God or Science. All disease is the punishment of our belief [opinion] either directly or indirectly, and our senses are what punishes us. My senses are attached to the Wisdom that sees through the opinion, so that my love or Wisdom or Truth casteth out their disease or fear; for their fear hath torment, and perfect wisdom casteth out all opinions. . . .

I am often accused of opposing the medical faculty and the religious creeds. In answer to this I plead guilty, but you must not gather from this that I oppose goodness or virtue. I oppose all religion based on the opinions of men, and as God never gave an opinion I am not bound to believe that man's opinions are from God. The difference between man's opinions and God's wisdom is more than one would naturally suppose, but the former is taken for a truth. This makes the trouble with which the wise have to contend. If a man knew himself he would not be misled by the opinions of others, and *as disease is the result of our opinions it is the duty of us all to know ourselves, that we may correct our own errors.* Now if error is something to correct it must require more wisdom than the knowledge which invented it. When I find a person diseased I know his trouble must have a father or beginning. Just because it is ignorant of its father, do not supposed that it is without a father. So to destroy your earthly father is to destroy your opinions, and to be with your heavenly Father is to be wise; so that everyone that loses his opinions and arrives at the truth is dead to the natural world, but alive to Wisdom or Christ.

When I sit down by a sick person and he or she wants to tell me what the doctor says, to me, it is all nonsense, for I have not the least regard for their knowledge. Their opinions are what I try to destroy, and if I succeed their opinions have no power to create disease. A medical man's profession, not his wisdom, is the standard of his popularity. I stand in direct opposition to all others in this respect and *here is the conflict, whether man's opinion is to rule or his wisdom.* If the medical profession is based on wisdom, then it will stand the test, and disease must have its origin outside of the profession; either this must be true or the opposite. *I assert that disease is the offspring of opinion.*

You often hear persons attempt to explain my cures by their own opinions. Thus they make themselves out wise by their own ignorance, since they deny the very power of wisdom which they acknowledge by admitting it as a mystery to them. So they admit a power outside of their knowledge and worship that of which they are completely ignorant. Now I know that this something which is a mystery to them is wisdom to me and that my wisdom sees through their opinions; and also that the explanation is the conversion from an opinion to truth or health. The two characters, wisdom and opinion, stand before each other and the people choose the one they will obey.

Disease is the offspring of error and as long as the people worship men's opinions, just so long will they be sick. To me it is perfectly plain that *if the people could see themselves they would discard all the priests' and doctors' opinions and become a law unto themselves.* All I do is to put the world into possession of a wisdom that will keep them clear from these two classes of opinions. You may think I have some feeling against the character of the physicians but this is not so. Neither do I think that they who know me have anything against me as a man, but they scout the idea that I do not know any more about how I cure disease than anyone else; they think they have the wisdom, but I, somehow, have a healing power. I stand to the medical faculty in the light of a harmless humbug, perfectly ignorant of what I profess to know, and all my talk being to amuse the patients and make them believe that disease is in their imagination. If I succeed in doing this it is all well, but so far as wisdom goes, that is folly. I am aware that this is my position with the faculty and their opinions have such a strong hold on the people that most of them look upon me in the same light, and if by chance someone chooses to see that I am not the person these blind guides call me, they in time are looked upon in the same light. I acknowledge that all this is true with regard to my position in society, and how I feel in regard to it? I know that it is all false, although my word does not prove it so, but I suppose I have the same right to give my opinion with regard to these two classes as they have to give their opinions about me and I will now give it and let the masses judge for themselves.

Show me the doctor that really thinks his medicine has any curative qualities or any intelligence except as it is associated with his opinion and I will show you a fool. There are certain drugs that will act as a cathartic; but that only goes to show that because of error in the mind the body must be helped by something that will counter act the effect of the minds error. If error directs, nothing certain is known of the effect. If wisdom is at the helm no medicine is wanted, for Wisdom can break opinions in pieces.

Ignorance, which is in the belief that the body's health can be diseased by something outside of itself, identifies with the world's wisdom, which Jesus called foolishness, and truth is made a stranger while *the mind is all the time fighting against itself to get rid of an enemy of its own creation.* Now teach men this simple fact and their happiness will be the result.

OUTLINES OF
A NEW THEORY FOR CURING DISEASE

All medical practice claims that their mode of treatment is the best; yet no one has even hinted or dares to risk his reputation on the ground that disease is an invention of man and ought to be treated as an error or deception forced upon mankind by ignorance and superstition. My theory is that all phenomena called disease are the result of false beliefs originating in the darkness of Egyptian superstition.

Disease is what follows a belief and a belief is like an atmosphere so universal that everyone is liable to be affected by it as by chilly winds. How often we hear this remark, "Don't expose yourself to the damp, cold air or you will get a cold?" This belief is completely false, but when this cloud of thought is felt all persons, old and young, are affected, for the fear is the punishment of the belief. Science is the sun that burns up the clouds or changes the beliefs of man, and a little ray of intelligence springs up and the cloud of superstition vanishes, as the true God appears. The people will hail the truth, as they hail the rising sun long before it is seen on the horizon of the common minds.

DISEASE

What is disease? It is false reasoning. True scientific wisdom is health and happiness. False reasoning is sickness and death; and on these two modes of reasoning hang all of our happiness and misery. The question is, how can we know how to separate the one from the other? The truth cannot be changed; the false is always changing. The one is science, and the other is error, and our senses are attached to the one or the other. Science is the natural development of matter or mind, disease is the natural inventions of error. To show how disease is not what we suppose it to be I must show the absurdity of error's reasoning, for error is the father of disease.

We are all taught by error to call disease something that is independent of man. To make it more plain and show where the two modes of reasoning act, I will suppose a case and take that of a young man who feeling a little disturbed calls on a physician. The physician sounds his lungs, examines his heart, and tells the patient he is very liable to have heart-disease. The patient asks what he did to get the disease and is told that disease exists independent of anything the patient did. He is led to believe that even if he should die it would exist the same and others would be liable to get it. At last the patient really has the heart-disease, which his physician described to him.

Now imagine that you are the patient. Have you created the disease yourself or has the doctor created it for you? "I say you made it yourself.

Now to cure you is to show you that all the feeling you had at the commencement arose from a trifling cause, and that when I can make you understand it I have performed the cure." Instead of giving medicines or going to work by guess to destroy the disease, I commence by showing the patient how he framed it by his own hand. So I reason in this way: "You listened to the doctor to try and understand what caused heart-disease. He explained every variety of feeling or symptom, and you listened until you understood it. Now without knowing it you created in your mind the disease, as much as you would if an artist or mechanic had taught you how to draft a building, and you should carry in your mind the building and in your sleep create it. The only difference would be that one would please you, for it would contain wisdom, while the other would hinder you, for it would contain fear and would threaten to destroy your life. Your trouble is the material with which to build the building. *A chemical change in the fluids of your system takes place, governed by your belief, and you condense the changes into a phenomenon corresponding with your plan.* Your ingenuity in manufacturing the disease has been the destruction of your happiness. To destroy the disease I convince you that what the doctor said was an idea gotten up by error. Then not knowing how to account for some disturbance, which in itself amounted to nothing, you were led astray into the darkness of heathen superstition where all kinds of evil spirits and disease dwell in the brain of man. Superstition always shows itself through the ignorance of man's reasoning, assuming as many names and forms as the father of all lies allows.

WHAT DO I IMPART TO MY PATIENTS?

The question is often asked of me, do you impart anything to your patients when you talk? I answer, I do, and I will try to make you understand how. To do this I must give you an illustration. Suppose you are purchasing goods, and in your hurry you lose your wallet containing all your money. You do not miss it till you go to pay your bills, and then you find you have lost your cash. Now the shock excites your system or mind and you become excited and very nervous. This is accompanied by a feverish state of body, *for the bodily condition is only the reflection of the state of the mind.* At last you let your trouble be known to some person who helps you look for the money. You can't find it, and borrow money to pay the person for assisting you. This adds to the trouble, and at last you take to your bed and send for a physician. He feels of the pulse, says your head is affected, and gives you some medication. This only aggravates the nervous excitement, so you keep on till you finally give up and dismiss all the doctors and come to call on me. I know nothing of the trouble, but have found a wallet containing $1,000 and am going to advertise it. At the sight of the wallet you are startled and say, "that is mine." The shock changes the mind and the cure is made. Now who or what imparted the cure? It was the $1,000 I gave you. So this is the way I cure. The person has lost something that he cannot find or has gotten into some trouble he cannot get rid of. He wants something to satisfy his desires, and whatever that is, it is the same as the money, and the one who can impart it gives him the remedy. Suppose a person receives a shock from falling into a river and returns home with a state like a cold. This produces a cough. Now, as there are many ghosts in the form of disease, he fears some of them may get hold of him. So he goes to a doctor and lays his case before him. The doctor says to him, "You are very likely to have a cold." Now of course he is troubled, like the man who was looking for his lost money. So he inquires of every person what is good for a cough and every person gives his opinion, and there is just as much in one opinion as another. At last in despair he gives it up and I am sent for. I tell him what he is afraid of and how it is effecting him. Here is something he can't get from the doctor. This makes him feel more comfortable. Then I go on to show him how he has been living on opinions about an idea that has no existence except in the superstition of people. I have thus given him something in the form of truth that will dissolve the error and satisfy him.

MIND AND DISEASE

Men create ideas which are spiritual matter. These ideas have a real existence in the spiritual world, and their power is according to the strength of man's belief in them and the fear men have of them. Fear of an idea created by its creator can concentrate its spiritual matter to the point where it can be seen even by the natural eye; a creation composed of the loathsome characteristics conceived of by the person's own belief, an offspring of an excited and degraded mind. Such an idea is disease. This *disease was first one simple, uncompounded idea. But when that finally was pushed into an identity, when men were once afraid of it, then it grew rapidly, like a poisonous weed, and derived its sustenance from the very life-blood to which it owed its existence.* All its horrible characteristics it draws from the mind of men, who, if they only understood what they are doing, would plant a good seed in their soil or mind, which would bear no fruit fit for disease to live on, and thus it would starve to death. . . . *As mind makes spiritual matter, so it can annihilate it.*

In order that a disease shall be created, a shock must first be produced. You cannot move anything unless you first start it. There must be a shock, be it ever so slight, a little excitement, fright, pleasure, anything which would produce a disturbance in the system. When thus disturbed, the natural heat of the body always either increases or diminishes. Suppose you turn red. A stranger meets you and says you look flushed. That would not be likely to take down your color but would increase it. After two or three remarks of that kind you would begin to feel uncomfortable, your head would feel hot, and the heat might be so great that you would have pain, and presently you would be informed that you look feverish. That would keep up the excitement, and when you went out of doors you would be likely to cough from the irritation caused by the upward tendency of the heat. That would frighten you a little, though you might not own it or know it. But the disturbance would keep up till some kind friend should inform you that you had taken on a cold, for your face was flushed and you coughed. That, mind you, is an opinion, for a person may flush and cough from excitement without any cold at all. Now you only need a little help from mistaken friends and a finishing touch from a doctor to put you into a lung, brain, or any other kind of fever they please. That, to use a very simple case, is the way a disease is made.

Another example:

I lay my hand on my left side and you ask me what I feel. Now I am not sure what I feel, neither am I frightened. I would pass it off as without any means of any account, but you tell me that people often die with just such a feeling as I have. This startles me and your opinion troubles me exceedingly. I begin now to twist and turn, not knowing what to do. This convinces you that I have disease of the heart and you try to explain to me what I have and how it affects a person. *By your suggestions and strong opinions you disturb my mind and create the very idea you have invented, and at last I die just as you foretold. All this is disease and you made it. If I had never seen you nor anyone wiser than myself I should not have died.*

WHAT IS DISEASE

What is disease? This question involves much speculative reasoning. Some suppose that disease is independent of man; some think it is a punishment from God for the wrongs of our first parents; others that it comes from disobeying the laws of God. Now let us analyze the above and see if there is any truth in these statements.

According to man's reasoning disease is his enemy and if God created an enemy to destroy man, can God really be man's friend? Thus the idea that a benevolent God had anything to do with disease is a superstition; then the question comes up again, where does it come from?

My answer is: It does not come, it is created, not by God, but by man.

We have not a true idea of God. God is not a man any more than man is a Principle. When we speak of God we are taught to believe in a Person, so we attach our ideas to a Person called God and then talk about His laws and the violation of them is said to be our trouble. I have often heard it said: "If a man would obey all the laws of God he would never be sick." But when God's law is [deemed] so severe that man is liable to be made sick we sometimes imagine God to be a tyrant of the worst kind.

God is the name of a man's belief and our senses are attached to our opinions about our belief or God. The God of the savages is their belief; the God of the Mohammedans is their belief, and so on to the Christian's God. The Christian's God, like themselves, is like a house divided against itself. During the Civil War the God of the North and the God of the South were at war with each other as are the Christian worshippers today; each prays to God for help and each condemns the other. Thus it is plain that gods of this kind are a farce and all our worship of such is from a superstitious fear of a tyrant whose name we dare not take in vain.

The time will come when the true God will be worshipped in spirit and truth, for God is a Spirit and not a man. *Wisdom is the sower and God the vineyard, and as man is made in the image of God his [inner] mind is spirit and receives the seed of Wisdom.*

Wisdom has no laws, it is the true light. The law of man is the invention of evil thoughts. In proportion as Wisdom is in us the law is dead. So to be wise is to be dead to the law, for law is man's belief and Wisdom is of God or Science. Now if we could understand the true idea of causes and effects, we could learn where the true cause of disease originated.

Man has invented a God according to his belief so that God is the embodiment of man's belief. As man's belief changes so his God changes, but the true God never changes. The God of today was made up for the wisdom of the heathen world and we have revered and worshipped it not from love, but from fear. Its only opponent is the Science of Christ, so as Science enters this man made God gives way, but not without a struggle. The true God is not acknowledged by this man's God, but it is in the hearts of the people working like leaven till it leavens the whole lump. It is called by the children of this world of opinions infidelity. So to be an infidel is to question the God of man's opinions. Jesus saw through all this hypocrisy, that the God of the heathen was not the God of peace, but of war, and this same false God is worshipped now as then. He is called on now more than he has ever been since the Civil War. He is the most convenient God I know of. He listens to the North and the South and leads his followers into battle against each other. All this sort of cant is kept up with a certain solemnity of form as though there were real truth in it, but the time will come when all this must give way to a higher worship, for it is a vain worship that shows itself in every church in Christianity. They worship what they know not. This false idea is the foundation on which the Christian world stands and the waters that flow from this fountain are corrupt, for where the foundation is corrupt the stream is also. When the angel of truth disturbs the waters they throw forth every kind of corruption, this poisons the minds of the multitudes and makes them sick. *The true wisdom like the Science of Christ explains away this earthly God and brings man into a more happy state where opinions give way to facts.*

DISEASE – "WHAT IS THE CURE"

In the preceding article I asked the question, what is disease? And in that I gave the cause. Now I will describe how it is brought about and the cure. I said that man's God was the embodiment of man's belief or opinions. These opinions have been forced on man like burdens, till the people have had to yield to their weight and make the best of it. Yet they murmur and complain but dare not raise their voice in support of the God of wisdom. Opinions of themselves have no element of adhesion, therefore their life depends on coercion. So laws are established and penalties attached and if the people grumble, laws and penalties are applied, sanctioned by God, and you are told of the laws of God, while this same God is only the embodiment of their opinions reduced to a law. Disease is the result of disobeying these laws, so man is made to believe a lie that he may be condemned to disease.

For instance, some people believe that according to God's law, if we expose ourselves to cold air, or if we sit in a cold draft, we shall get a cold or become sick. Here God [supposedly] puts man between a rock and a hard place because sometimes man cannot help but be exposed to cold air or a draft and then is punished for it. But man thinks to himself, "If I expose myself I dare not find fault with God's punishment," therefore he lives all his life subject to a tyrant that will torment him for reasons he knows not of. This belief makes him a servant to sin and to man's opinion. So his life is in the hands of priests and doctors to be handled to suit their convenience. Thus man is a mere lump of clay in the hands of blind guides and whatever they say to the people they believe. Their beliefs disturb their minds and the doctors sow the seed of disease which they nurse till it grows to a belief, then comes the misery.

Now the God I worship has no fellowship with man's opinions, so to cure the disease is to break in pieces his opinions. This places man on his own wisdom, independent of man's God or opinions. Then he sees the one living and true God who rewards everyone according to the truth he understands. To know this God is to know ourselves and that is the religion of Christ. *It is Christ in us, not opinions that we are in.* Just as we know this truth we are of and a part of God; then we become joint heirs of God and will be guided by the wisdom of the Father of all Truth. This purifies and cleanses our minds from all opinions and leads us into the Science of Christ where opinions never come.

We all have a God according to our belief. A belief contains no wisdom but is a shadow of something that cannot be seen, worshipped by man who knows not what it is. This something is what the world of opinions reasons about. The Jews prophesied about it, looking for its coming as for a man of great power who would free them from the Roman yoke. Heathen nations had a vague idea of this something. They incorporated it into their beliefs as a monarch or king. So it has always been in the world or in man's belief, but man knows it not. Even to the wise it is a stranger. It has no place in their hearts or in the religious world except as an unexplained mystery. It comes to man's senses but man knows it not. It stands knocking at the door but it is not recognized as having an identity; *so it is mocked at, spit upon, hated and despised by all men.* Yet it is always the same, calm and unmoved, sympathizing with its friends, who are bound down by the opinions of this world's belief.

Now, what is it? It is an invisible Wisdom which can never be seen by the eye of opinion, for when the truth comes the opinion or matter is seen to be the shadow of this Light or Substance that I call something. Again, what is it? If I should tell you what it is you would ask for proof, but my proof would be from my opinion, so I will give the proof of it from *your own opinion*. Still what is it?

It is what never has been acknowledged to have an identity.

Then what is it that has been admitted but cannot be seen and yet is not acknowledged to have an identity?

Can the reader answer? "Yes, it is God."

I ask, Is God without an identity?

You say no.

Then it is not God.

What then is it?

I will try and tell you and bring the opinions of the world to prove my answer. It is the key that unlocks the innermost secrets of the heart in the prison of man's belief, and it frees the prisoner who has been bound and kept from good health. Opinions are like a shadow of the substance called God. True wisdom is attached to the substance Itself; false wisdom is attached to the shadow. Language is attached to the shadow, which is attached to the substance; when language is not in harmony with wisdom the discord lies in opinion. If the senses are attached to opinion, when the opinion is lost man loses his opinion but not his senses or life, for his life is in his wisdom or self-existence, not in his opinions.**

This something, which I have called Substance or the Science of Christ, is a knowledge of this wisdom which puts man in possession of a truth that he can explain to another. It does not come to the man of opinions. This shows that every man has two selves, one acknowledged by the natural man, the other by the spiritual man. Here is the proof.

To give the proof I must make the reader detach his senses from a God of man's belief and attach them to this invisible Wisdom which fills all space, and whose attributes are all light, all wisdom, all goodness and love, which is free from all selfishness and hypocrisy, which makes or breaks no laws, but allows man to work out his own salvation; which holds men responsible for their belief, right or wrong, without respect to persons. For the natural man is only a shadow of man's wisdom, and the shadow from this world of opinions will be destroyed when the light of the Wisdom comes, but the life will be saved, for when the senses are attached to this Wisdom, then shall be brought to pass that saying, "Oh! death! where is thy sting! Oh, grave! where is thy victory!" Death is robbed of its victim, the grave gives up its idea of death. Then life rises to that happy state where death, hell, and disease and the torments of existence find no place, from whence no traveler ever returns but where man knows himself. This wisdom teaches him that when our senses are attached to opinions of any kind we become the subject of that opinion and suffer according to the penalty attached to it, unless forgiven or the debt paid by the truth.

This is the new truth spoken of by Jesus; to know this is to have eternal life and the life is the wisdom that can enter the dark prisons of man's mind and find his life imprisoned by the opinions of this world and there hear his groans, feel his sorrows and break the prison walls of his belief and set him free. When a person professes this Wisdom and attaches his life to it, his life is to him a blessing, for it is of use to mankind. Then he is happiest when relieving those who have fallen into trouble, or into the hands of thieves who have them robbed of their substance and those imprisoned in a creed, there to languish from the wounds of the priests and doctors till the angel of Wisdom or the tide of progress shall beat against the walls of this superstition and break down the medical opinions, lay priest-craft low and overflow the superstitious world with the Science of Christ and good order. Then all men will be judged by what they know and all can prove themselves by this standard.

**The Kingdom of Heaven is the result of having no opinions. We live and move within the Kingdom of Heaven, but we are unaware of its presence when we have opinions. Our opinions make a pseudo world in which we live.

WISDOM IS PROVEN BY ITS WORKS

Every science has its standard, based on actual knowledge, not on opinion. The two most dangerous opinions to the happiness of man are those of medical science and the priests. These two classes are the foundation of more misery than all other evils, for they have such a strong hold on the minds of the people by their deception and cant. They claim all the virtue and wisdom of the nation, and have so deceived the people that their claims are acknowledged in war and peace. Let us question the beliefs of these guides.

Yes, they have a semblance of truth in them, but is the world made wiser or better by them?

Are not their opinions like the locusts of Egypt in everything you eat and drink? Science and progress have had to fight both theories ever since the world began to think and act.

Religion was what crucified Christ. Pilate's wisdom found no fault with Him, but the religion of the priests said "crucify him." Paul had this idea of religion when he said to the Athenians, "I perceive you are altogether too religious or superstitious." Then he goes on to show them how their religion led them to worship this something of which I am talking, so he said, "This something that you so ignorantly worship, I declare unto you." Here you see that Paul was not a religious man, but was converted from a man of religious and superstitious opinions to a man of science and progress and he showed that this something was not far off, though the religious world did not know it. And the world will never know it till wisdom separates religion and medicine from the scientific world. All Science is spiritual and is not known by the priests and doctors. The theories of these two classes are not based on wisdom but on opinions. Wisdom is the solid or substance. *Matter or mind is the shadow of the spirit of real wisdom.* Now put man in possession of this wisdom so that he can make an application of it for the benefit of the suffering community and then this wisdom will separate the chaff from the wheat.

TRUTH AND ERROR - THE TWO PRINCIPLES

All Jesus' parables were intended to illustrate the two principles, truth and error. Truth is the wisdom of God; error is the god of opinions, and the two have no dealing with each other. Each has his disciples, but their acts are so different that their characters can be easily explained. I will give you the religious or political god. He is represented as watching the movements of the armies and dictating to the heads of the nation. No one approaches him except the ordained priest. He takes particular care of the president and the heads of departments, in fact he is ruler and dictator of all things. But he must be approached with as much reverence as a king.

Now where is the God in whose wisdom I believe? He is in the hearts of the people. He is not a man, neither has He form. He is neither male nor female. I will give you an illustration of His wisdom. If you see a man in trouble are you required to help him. No! but if the Christ lives within you, you will want too and you will be rewarded because you want to. This embraces the law and the gospel, and on this hangs all man's happiness and misery. If man is governed by this truth, it develops his higher wisdom and enables him to prove all things by a standard based not on opinions but on truth. All man's happiness or misery is in keeping or breaking this law of love.

Now if a man is in trouble and you help him, out of duty to the law, rather than out of love, you will have no reward. Also, you will have no reward if you are helping because you think you will get a reward. ..... This higher law is the most perfect of all laws. It is very little understood, and not at all intelligently. To understand it intelligently is to make it your rule of action with the sick, or those in trouble.

HOW THOUGHTS MAKE ILLNESS

I will make an illustration to show how our mind and senses interact to make illness.

Suppose you are ignorant of the effects of a charcoal fire. You sit down in a room and the heat affects your mind and body. As more coals are added you become hotter and hotter; all this contains no intelligence. In like manner opinions enter life and like hot coals the more you add the more heat or anxiety you add to you life. Reason which is another element of fire fans the flames till life and the senses are so affected that they are burned by the heat. This is disease.

Now, suppose I come in as the healer; The heat instantly affects my intuitive mind and my wisdom communicates to my senses [consciousness] the cause and the remedy. My senses become composed, my wisdom directs my senses, and they act on the patient; the door is opened, the trouble is explained, the patient is saved from his torment, his mind or wrong opinion is changed or destroyed, but his life is saved and his trouble is at an end. *Opinions are the elements that come to torment life or the senses*, yet they contain no wisdom above the brute and can be destroyed. All the opinions of the priests are collected and condensed into a solid substance according to their belief, and although they cannot be seen by the natural eye, the eye of truth or science can see them and lead the senses that are attached to the opinion to the locality where the beliefs are and correct them there. For instance, the priests tell their hearers that there is another world separate from this one. They give such a glowing account of it that their opinions, like fuel, set fire to the hearers and a chemical change takes place in their minds; their minds are disturbed and their senses are affected by the opinions of the priests and then so called professionals are sent out into the world to fix the problems actually created by the priests' opinions. The minds are so disturbed that the life, losing its relish for this world, is persuaded to embark for the world of the priests' opinions, to which their thoughts are attached. Their senses are held between two opinions, not knowing what to do; this is called by the doctors "disease of the mind or mental illness." They, not knowing the cause of the trouble, are ready to be deceived by the ignorance of the doctor. So the doctor, like the priest, sets up a false idea of disease and engrafts into the patient's belief a new idea of some disease which affects the body. Then he reasons till it takes root in the mind and comes forth in the image of its father. The life or senses are then attached and the thing is brought to the doctor to receive a name. So after he examines it and gives it the name of cancer, the patient wants to know what is to be done. The doctor gives the treatment of such a disease, which often seems more like a torture than the disease itself; this troubles the patient who wants to leave the opinions of the doctor or cancer and escape to the priests' world where they are told that through prayer diseases may be overcome. Here they are halted between two opinions; this last stand causes a real disease of the body for now reason is brought to inflame the mind and the patient is disturbed and overrun with false theories.

THE DARKNESS OF SUPERSTITION

The enemies of Christ Science and progress are mustering everyone into their prisons of belief. But I enter this land of darkness with the light of liberty, search out the dungeons where the lives of the sick are bound, enter them and set the prisoners free.

I have said all diseases are opinions condensed into an idea of spiritual matter that can be seen by the eye of Wisdom. In like manner all ideas of the priests can be seen and each throws off its shadow, and each has its particular odor so that it can be detected as easily by the senses of Wisdom as an apple or an orange can be detected by the sense of smell.

To be in a teacher of this unknown God is what has been acknowledged by the opinions of man. Thousands of persons have undertaken to penetrate this land of mystery and have returned with the idea that they háve made the discovery and thus have deceived themselves and many people, broken up families, and led the weak, until the people, like the children of Israel, have left their happy land or state of mind to follow these blind guides, and they have wandered so far from health or home that they have lost their way and fallen among strangers, priests, and doctors, who pretending to be their friends have robbed them of their happiness and left them like the prodigal son sick and disheartened in this land of superstition.

Like Moses, I enter this land [wilderness] and lead them out, and as I pass through the sea of blood or beliefs of those blind guides I feed them with the bread of wisdom and smite the rock of truth and the water or wisdom gushes out and cools the parched tongues. I go before them in this wilderness, holding up the flag of freedom and all that listen to my explanation are healed from the bite of false creeds. The people murmur and complain, some call me humbug and quack; others want to return to their old ideas of religion, but I stand up and entreat them, stimulating them to press forward and not to give up till I have restored them once more to the happy land of health whence they have been decoyed away. So I am hated by some, laughed at by others, spit upon by the doctors, and sneered at by the priest, but received into the arms of the sick who know me.

SUMMARIZING THE JOURNEY

Perhaps by this time it would be well to sum up all this journey, describing how I entered this land [wilderness] and how I passed through it. I will do so in a few words.

After I found that mind was spiritual matter I found that its ideas were also spiritual matter condensed into a solid called disease, and that this, like a book, contained all the wisdom of its author. Seeing the book (for sight with Wisdom embraces all senses, hearing, tasting, etc.) I open it and read through it. To the patient it is a sealed book but to Wisdom there is nothing hid which cannot be revealed or seen, nor so far off that it cannot be reached. So I read the contents of the book to the patient and show that it is false, then, as the truth changes his mind light takes the place of darkness, till he sees through the error of disease. The light of Wisdom dissipates the spiritual matter or disease and the patient once more finds himself freed of opinions and happiness is restored.

Disease is nothing but an opinion taken for a substance and the misery comes from mistaking the opinion for a truth. Now let the people understand that there is no wisdom in an opinion, and let them cease from giving opinions, and you will shut the mouths of these barking dogs, howling night and day, which keep the people in constant excitement.

THE CHRISTIAN'S GOD

I will now introduce the Gods of the two opposing theories. One of them is only man's opinion, the other is truth. In the first theory religion is the father, medicine is the son, and law is the Holy Ghost, or explanation. These three make up the God of our superstitious belief. These give the people their beliefs, which are sanctioned by an appearance of divine wisdom, and according to their belief acknowledged by the wisdom of the father of all. Strange as this may seem, it is the foundation of all the misery that man suffers. Although we are taught to love and respect this man's God as the giver of everything we receive, yet if one half of what we attribute to Him were true He would be of all tyrants the worst. If we should look upon a parent as we are taught to look upon God, we should hate our parents. Let us see what kind of God He is and how He compares with a parent.

In the first place, He is represented as knowing all our acts and having a watchful care over us like a good father. Now if any parent could have half the power that they say God has over His children and would allow such pain and suffering, His children would curse Him to his face. Now all this talk about a God who reasons and makes bargains accompanied by rewards and punishments is so much like the natural man's wisdom that no one can help seeing that our Christian God is no more than the embodiment of man's belief when man was at the beginning of his evolutionary process and very undeveloped. His concept of God is spoken of in the likeness of a military officer, or some grand monarch, or king. He is king of kings, the great High Priest. Once it was the height of honor to be a military officer, for that was the greatest of all professions; therefore God must be a military character, for the Bible says He had war in heaven. The devil was the first secessionist we find and he was driven out of heaven. You never hear God compared to a statesman or any learned man.

When Jesus came to earth many years ago, since He was not represented as a military character, but instead was spiritually wise and compassionate and caring, they had no claim on Him, so the wise of this world who base their theory on opinions had Him crucified and stole His ideas and engrafted them into their aristocratic creeds. This kept them aloof from the masses and the people were taught that God would only communicate to them through the priests.

We all really believe more of this than we are willing to acknowledge and it keeps us in bondage under the priests. This burden of false ideas makes men nervous and superstitious. This gets their systems in a condition for another swarm of hungry dogs called doctors who invent diseases, make the people believe their opinions, and after their opinions are believed then they are ready to bring about any disease that can be introduced to them. As people cannot see how disease is made, this false theory has always led the people and always will until the true idea of how disease is made is explained. According to my theory, all errors can be explained on scientific truths, so that man can be his own doctor and priest. According to my theory, mind can be changed and any kind of an idea produced. So apply this truth to the mind, and you can cure or correct the error and establish the truth.

\

JESUS AND TRUTH

What truth did Jesus come to bring to the world? One simple fact that man is a progressive being, that his happiness and misery are of his own making, that his belief is his wisdom and if founded on an opinion it will make him unhappy and sick. To separate the truth from the error is a Science the knowledge of which teaches how to correct an error or disease, and in this knowledge is eternal life. Jesus' words and acts showed them that their beliefs were false, and that they were the cause of their misery, but this they could not understand, and being in their belief, their belief became part of their identity. As they were taught to believe in spirits their misery was attributed to them, and as error begets error the people were tormented by their own beliefs. It never entered into the minds of these blind leaders that as a man sows so shall he reap; that action and reaction are equal. *Knowledge of science was not general, and the possibility that the belief of man had anything to do with his health was not dreamed of.* All that was believed was something that could not be seen, so the prophets prophesied of someone coming from the heavens. Now if heaven had not been something that people believed in away and apart from this earth it would not have been in the prophecies. So this heaven was an established fact and all their controversies were in regard to it. They introduced all sorts of mediums who were reported to have come from and to have communication with that place. Heaven was the dwelling of God and all religious theories were based upon the belief that there was another world where God dwelt and where He ordered all things according to His own will. Absurd as this is, a man is made of this composition of beliefs, for man is only a mass of ideas combined together by a wisdom superior to the matter of which the ideas are formed.

Science is not recognized in this belief for it belongs to that class of minds which have never risen to a state where they can discern that man can perceive anything independently of his natural senses. To this class of minds whatever is not established is a mystery. If a lead ball is thrown into the water it sinks to the bottom, that is a fact; if a wooden ball is also thrown into the water it floats, and then comes the mystery. A medium from the other world is required to explain the phenomenon; argument is of no force, the explanation must come from God, and thus it is with every mysterious phenomenon: supernatural power only can explain it. Thus man is kept constantly excited to understand every little thing that happens. *He never has thought that heaven and hell were part of his belief and consequently part of himself, but he believes that these two places are independent of himself and he is liable to go to one or the other after he is dead. So he lives in hell all his life trying to get to heaven, but he never gets there for it is always at a distance, and he is looking for a savior to save him from hell.*

How often we hear very good people say that they are weary of this wicked world and long to be with Christ, showing that they are not with Him now but hope to be. Their faith contains a belief, not a substance. The faith that is of man is merely a belief in something not obtained, for when the substance is obtained their faith or belief is lost in the substance, and they have what they hope for. Jesus' faith was the substance of our belief and that substance was Christ. The Christ or faith is intended to be applied to man, and Jesus put this in practice for our happiness. The question arises, has the Christ an identity? I answer it has; it is all that ever had an unchangeable identity, it is Wisdom itself. But the Christian's faith is an opinion about this Wisdom. I have said that *the faith of Jesus had an identity and to this His senses were attached.* Then Jesus could say to His faith, "Father forgive them, for they know not what they do."

What did this Christ strive to do? It strove to enter the heart of man and teach him to break away from his errors and learn the truth. *Jesus taught Christ and put it in practice by His words.* Do the Christians do the same? No, they preach about it. So their faith is not of works but a belief. The world is no wiser or better for it. To prove your faith in music is to play a tune on an instrument by your faith or science, not to talk about music, telling how beautiful it is. The Science of Health which Jesus taught was practiced by His faith or wisdom, and His instrument was man.

How does Jesus stand by the side of His pretended followers? He talked and taught His Christ to the people, priests and doctors talk about it. Here is a vast difference. Jesus put intelligence in the Christ or Science; the Christians put no intelligence in Christ or Science, but apply all the intelligence to Jesus, calling the Christ a "power." This difference has always been kept up; the natural man cannot see intelligence in anything he cannot understand, therefore Christ or the intelligence of Jesus is to him a mystery, and he wants to know whence it came. This ignorance on the part of the priests and the people originated all this speculation about Jesus. The Christ or higher intelligence to them was shrouded in darkness, for they could not see why He, merely a man, should be more than a man.

Everyone knows that an intuitive state is different from the natural state. Let me illustrate what all will admit. Persons in an intuitive state can talk, using the same organs as when awake, they also have every faculty which they possess in the waking state, but they act independently of the natural body or identity of flesh and blood.

Now where is the identity when the natural man is acting, for both cannot be acting at the same time? *Everyone will perceive that if a man could retain his reason and natural senses, and at the same time be conscious of the other state* **he would be a man beside himself**, *thus having two living intelligences in one* *identity acting through one [organism]. Thus the intuitive man man could correct the errors of the man of the flesh and blood and keep him in subjection to his wisdom.*

This is my state as far as regards the sick. When I sit by the sick and take a patient by the hand I feel a sensation. This excites the spiritual or scientific man, and his higher senses being free from matter or opinions see the natural man with his opinion that causes the trouble. As I retain two identities I see the error and explain it to the natural senses. These are set at rest and harmony is restored. I cannot find language to explain this so that you will fully understand it.

LOVE

What is the element that receives all sensation? Love for ourselves. This is the groundwork or foundation of all our acts. It is the mortar or dough in which all sensation is made. Of itself it contains no knowledge, it is perfect harmony; its elements or language is its perfection. It embraces all the senses; it is not Wisdom but the power Wisdom uses to bring all things into harmony with itself. To this world of ignorance it is not known, yet the matter or ideas of this world are put into this element. Like the ocean it can hold all sorts of ideas, be disturbed to its lowest depths and then calmed by Wisdom so that not a ripple on the surface can be seen. But in the depth of this ocean of love lie all sorts of error that are gnawing at the life of the soul and are identified with it; this is the disease in the mind.

When the storm of ignorance and superstition was raging and all the ships or minds were tossing to and fro, even Jesus' disciples were in danger of being swamped by the errors of the age: when their ship or belief was just going down into heathen idolatry and their enemies disturbed their water or belief, in the darkness of the night of error, when there was no eye to see nor heart to feel, no arm to reach out nor voice to be heard, Christ or Truth was seen walking upon their waters or belief, saying to the waves 'Be still!" And the wind and waves obeyed Him and there was a great calm.

Now the people are divided into two classes, followers of Christ and followers of Jesus. To illustrate the difference between Jesus and Christ I will take myself. There are many persons who believe in my "power" of healing, they call it the Quimby Power, but they know nothing of the truth of it. So I stand before the people judged according to my outward acts, by one class and by my Science by another; so if I should put on the cloak of hypocrisy, attend church and be very strict in all things pertaining to the wisdom of the world, I should be received by the wisdom of this world, but the scientific would look upon me as a hypocrite. Jesus' private character as a man had just as much to do with Christ as Quimby has to do with his cures. Jesus as a man knew nothing of Christ, neither does Quimby as a man know anything of this Wisdom or Truth, but when he feels it he speaks not as Quimby, but as the patient's troubles reveal it to him. This Science of Quimby takes the sins or troubles and the answer is accompanied by the feelings. Thus Quimby is the medium of the Truth to correct the errors of the world, just as Jesus was the medium of God or Science to convince man of his errors and lead him to Christ, health, or Truth.

I will take myself as a figure. Suppose music had never been reduced to a science and I had discovered that it could be taught to others, and I undertook to teach it, and I called the Science, Christ. Then it would be Quimby's Christ or theory. Suppose you should try to learn it so as to teach it. Would my Christ or theory have anything to do with my character as a man? All will say, no. If I am a very good man, that has nothing to do with my science, only to make it more admired, or it might make persons give more heed to what I say. Now suppose I am as bad a man as I can be, does that prevent me from teaching my Christ or Science? Of course we should prefer a person who is amiable and pleasant, if he is a teacher of any science, but it is not necessary that he should be a good or a bad man. So far as Jesus stands I do not pretend to be or not to be a disciple of Jesus, for I let my life and acts as a man speak for themselves. I do not pin my belief on Jesus' character, nor do I care anything about it anymore than He did Himself. Like all men who are willing to be judged by their acts, He let His character speak for itself. It was the Christ that Jesus was proud of, and so all men ought to be proud of any science that would make the world wiser and better. I profess to be a disciple of Christ, not of Jesus or the man. I let my man speak for himself, but I believe in Christ, which I put in practice on all those who live in this world of misery without this Science. So all my prayers are offered to Christ, not Jesus. The world prays to Jesus, but Jesus prayed to God to forgive or teach them, for they knew not what they prayed to. Now this Christ is an element of love that contains no error.** It is an element of pure love that will wash away all error that chances to get into it. It knows no evil, it sees no wrong in itself, it is perfect harmony and attraction. It contains our higher senses. So it is as it were our life, and all that is good and harmonious. The wisdom of Christ seeks to understand the world of error as a means of correcting it. Its happiness is the developing of God's love or Science, it analyzes all misery and trouble to liberate the soul that is bound in this world of error.

**Christ is an element of love that contains our higher spiritual senses. Our higher senses can see error, but experience only Truth. Christ Science is that which has always been, has never changed, and will never change.

JESUS' HEALING AND HIS MISSION

Why should there be such a controversy in regard to the way in which Jesus cured disease, also what was the real object of His mission in this world? These questions naturally arise in the minds of men and bring up doubts. By some it is believed that Jesus came to save man from being lost in another world and it is thought that He intended to reform the world. All admit He had a gift superior to other men but what it was has never been ascertained. The same controversy is going on today, and in fact it has always been a mystery to the natural man. Phenomena are taking place everywhere proving this power or gift and all admit it, but as yet it has not been reduced to a science, so it has never been explained. If it is a gift or power, why should He be called God or anything else above His followers? And if Jesus knew how He wrought miracles it is knowledge and not a gift, and to call it a gift or power is depriving Jesus of any knowledge superior to His followers. When it is recognized as a Science that Jesus taught for the happiness of man, man will try to learn it.

Then the inquiry will be made, how can it be proved a Science?

I answer, never till the people admit [recognize] that matter and mind are under direction of Intelligence superior to both. Then man will take a higher standard and be governed by Science, not mind. When mind becomes subject to Christ Science, which is spiritual power put into motion, then through this medium matter can be changed into any form or state.

I will give an illustration: Suppose a person believes he has a tumor in his left side. His error believes in the idea of tumors independent of his mind; he then allows his error to develop. His mind gives direction to matter and the idea is formed; this seems to be proof that there is such a thing as a tumor. No one will recognize that this is a phenomenon brought about by false knowledge, and that true knowledge or Science can destroy that tumor or idea and establish a knowledge of the truth that will prevent the person from being deceived into that error again . . . *Our bodies [in relation to mind] are nothing but an idea of matter that is either under the control of error or false knowledge, or under the control of Science or true knowledge.* If Truth or Science reigns, all goes well; if error reigns the wage is death, for all acts of error lead to death; death is an idea or matter, and all the acts of Science destroy death and lead to life and happiness.

RELIGION and HEALTH

Religion is a belief and disease or happiness is what follows.

Jesus had no rituals or ceremonies but a love for a higher development of the human soul. This was Jesus' religion and He put it in practice by His acts upon the sick. Not by giving an opinion of what He knew nothing about, but by showing that their sickness was the effect of their belief.

How often have you heard persons say they never change their mind. That is as much as to say they have no wisdom, for wisdom changes the mind. It often happens that a belief, especially if it is a wrong belief, is an obstacle to wisdom. This obstacle must be removed before the truth can shine. If there is not wisdom enough to remove the obstruction we say such a man has a strong mind or is stubborn. Now let us contrast the difference between the strong-minded and the intellectual man. *One sees no way to remove the obstacle and concludes that it cannot be overcome and then settles down in the strength of his own mind, while the other investigates the chances and sets himself to work to remove the burden.* As the intellectual man works, his mind changes, while the strong man makes up his mind and nothing can change it. This is the case with disease. The belief in the disease is the burden to be overcome and only the mind of the intellectual man is flexible enough to change the belief causing the burden and thereby relieving it.

THE EFFECT OF RELIGION ON HEALTH

I will give my opinion of the inconsistency of our religious beliefs and their effect upon health. I was visiting a patient whose state differed very much from what is called rheumatism and general disability of the nervous system. The doctors had tried their best to relieve her but to no effect; their efforts only made her worse, and at last she sent for me. I found her very nervous, complaining of aches and pains all over.

When I told her that it was her mind that was disturbed, this is how she replied, *"Oh, no, my mind is at rest. I know I am in the hands of a merciful God who will deal with me according to His will. I have full faith in Him."*

Do you suppose He knows your troubles? I asked.

"Yes, He knows all things."

Suppose Jesus were here, as He was many years ago, do you think He could cure you?

"Oh, yes. I know He knows all my suffering."

Then why does He not cure you today?

"Because it is His will that I should go through all this suffering to fit me for the kingdom of heaven."

Now suppose your daughter should be taken sick away from home in a strange land among strangers and suppose a kind friend should call on her and say,

"You seem very low spirited" and she should reply,

"Oh, no I know that it is all right."

And suppose your friend would ask, "Does your mother know you are here so she can come and help make you well?"

And your daughter would answer, "Yes, she knows all my sufferings, but she knows it is all right because it will make me better prepared to enjoy her company when I get home."

"Do you believe that if she had a mind to cure you she could do so?"

"Certainly."

'"Can you say you love your mother when you admit your life is in her hands and she permits you to suffer so much?"

"Oh, she is my mother, and I feel that she knows what is for the best. It gives me comfort to know that I am in the hands of a merciful being such as her."

[Despite this reasoning the patient fails to admit a point, and so more questioning continues]

Would you like to have me cure you?

"Yes, if you can, but not if I must give up my belief in my religion. I should rather go down to the grave with my religion than be cured and lose my belief. If you can cure me of my lameness and not talk to me about my religion I should like to get well, but if you cannot cure me without that I do not know as I will be cured, for I don't think my religion has anything to do with my disease."

Do you not think your belief has something to do with your happiness?

"Oh, yes, but it has nothing to do with my disease."

What is your disease?

"Why, it is rheumatism, the doctors say, and a general prostration of the nervous system."

What is that?

"Neuralgia, I suppose."

What is that?

"I do not know."

Suppose I should try to explain how you came to be in this condition, would you listen?

"Yes, if you do not talk religion. I do not want to lose my religion. How about you Mr. Quimby, Do you have religion?"

Yes! I have religion, but I would not want it if it made me as sick and unhappy as you.

"All the comfort I take while lying here all these long nights is to think that I am in the hands of a merciful God who will do all things right."

Would you like to get well?

"If it is the will of God, I should be very glad to get well."

Do you think I can cure you?

"I do not know, but I hope you can; if you can't I shall give up all hopes of ever being well."

Then you think your health depends on my science?

"Yes."

If I should cure you would you give me credit?

"Oh, yes."

But would it be right to upset the will of God who is keeping you in this misery for His own purpose?

"Oh, if God sees fit to have it I believe it is all right. I know I feel badly and I should like to feel better, but if it is the will of God that I must suffer I will submit for I know it is for the best. God suffered in the flesh to teach us to be better prepared for heaven."

Then you think if you should die you would go to heaven?

"I hope so, for I cannot suffer these pains always."

Where is heaven? Do you believe it is a place?

"Oh, no."

Then what is it?

"It is a state of mind."

Then you are not very near it, I should judge by your own mind.

"Well, I do not know as that has anything to do with my pains."

What is pain?

"I don't know what it is, but I know how it feels."

How do you know it?

"I know it through my senses."

Are your senses affected by your mind?

"I suppose so."

Then if your mind is disturbed and you put a false construction on the disturbance, won't it produce an unpleasant effect upon the senses?

"I suppose so."

Suppose this unpleasant effect should be pain, is it not the effect produced on the mind?

"I don't know what that has to do with my lameness. I want to get well."

Who wants to get well?

"I do."

That is, you, Mrs. H who wants to get well ?

"Yes."

Is not what you call you your mind or knowledge [spirit]?

"Yes, I guess so."

You do not expect this flesh and blood to go to heaven?

"No."

Why not?

"Because the Bible says flesh and blood cannot inherit the Kingdom 'of Heaven."

I thought you just said heaven was a state of mind.

"So I did."

Well, do you mean that flesh and blood are in the mind?

"Oh, you make me so nervous, you will kill me."

Why?

"Because I don't like to hear you talk so. My mind is all made up and I do not want to be disturbed in this way."

Do you mean your flesh and blood are disturbed?

"Oh you disturb my mind and body."

Then you believe your mind is one thing and your body another.

I guess so!

Do you believe in the soul?

"Yes."

You believe it goes to heaven when you die?

"Yes."

I thought you said heaven was a state of mind.

"Oh, yes, but we must die."

What dies?

"This flesh and blood."

Well, has it life?

"Yes."

Has it feeling?

"You would think so if you suffered as much as I do."

Then this that suffers is the flesh and blood?

"Yes."

Then it is conscious of all these bad feelings?

"Yes."

Are the feelings its consciousness, or has it another consciousness independent of itself?

"I would say it does not have a consciousness independent of itself."

Then at death you think that all of these aches and pains leave you and you will be happy

"Yes."

Then these aches and pains are the body's identity and belong to the flesh and blood?

"Yes."

Are you happy when you feel so badly?

"No."

Then you are not in heaven, am I right?

"I don't expect to be happy until I get to heaven."

Can you get there and have these pains?

"No."

Then when the pains leave you it will be heaven on earth?

"Yes, if that ever takes place."

One last question, Do you believe that God plays favorites or judges people by their faith and actions?

"He judges them by their faith and action."

Now, let us see where you stand. You have admitted enough to show that your mind is in a confused state like a person in trouble. Your supposed knowledge is the effect of an impression on the senses, due to the opinion of someone who explained someone's ideas according to his own view of truth. This opinion taken for truth makes you nervous and brings about all your suffering. You pray to the God whom you admit keeps you in misery. You are taught to believe that God is watching all your actions, that He has laid down certain laws and regulations for you to follow and if you disobey you will be punished. This keeps you in bondage and all your life subject to disease. But to suppose God selects you to be punished above your companions is to believe God is partial. This you cannot believe.

Now look at those who worship God; they have a false idea of the God they worship. *God is not in any kind of worship that man has established.* God is not an identity as man is. This false idea keeps man in the dark. You never see a man praying to the fire that warms him, nor does he pray to the elements. It is the same with electricity? Is not the person who knows the most about electricity the best one to control it, and does not everyone have more confidence in such a person than in one who is ignorant of it? So it is with the elements. Man differs in one respect from other living things: he has undertaken to control the elements so as to make them subservient to his will.

We often hear people talking about the laws of nature, as though they were the laws of God and they say if we did not disobey them all would go right. Now, here is the mistake. The laws of nature are very simple of themselves and they never trouble man if he does not trouble them. The beasts conform to these laws, for when they are thirsty they find the laws that quench their thirst, if left to themselves, and when hungry the same intelligence dictates the remedy. But man in his eagerness to be lord over the brutes and elements has developed faculties called senses. These are under a superior wisdom which can control the elements and use them for the benefit of the human race. So it is with life. Life is a science that is little understood.

Our lives are like a journey through a wilderness. We first take the priests' opinion, that is, to trust in God. When we ask an explanation of God we are answered that He knows all things and not a hair of our head falls to the ground without God knowing it; if we look to Him, He will deliver us from all danger, and He takes better care of us than a parent does of his child. This is a brief sketch of God's goodness. Now suppose we should not do quite as well as we expect, then what follows? God has made a devil, a something worse that stands ready to catch us if we don't go according to His will or laws. These things are not defined so man can construe them according to his belief. The laws of God made by man are arbitrary, though not acknowledged as such. Jesus said "Call no man master but one and that is God." Here you see you have made a God that is full of inconsistencies and cannot stand the test of common reason. Now look at the true scientific answer to all our beliefs and it shows us that they contain no knowledge of God or life, for God is life eternal and this life was in His Son, Jesus, which was Christ or Science. Now to suppose you lose your life is to be cut off from God, for God is not the God of the dead but of the living, for all live to Him. Now destroy man's belief and introduce God's truth, then we are set free from this world of error and introduced into the world of light or Science, where there is no death but the living God. This Science will lead us to that happy state where there is no sickness, sorrow, or grief, where all tears are wiped away from our eyes, and there we shall be in the presence of this great Truth that will watch us and hold us in the hollow of its hand and will be to us a light that will open our eyes. We shall not then be deceived by blind guides who say peace, peace, when there is no peace. Then we shall call no one master or leader, for there is but One that leads us and that is God. He puts no restriction upon us, for our lives are in His hands or Science. . . . *If you can see God in your knowledge you will admit that everything you do intelligently you do under the direction of a power or intelligence superior to yourself. So when you do anything ignorantly and the effect is bad, giving you trouble, you try to correct your errors, thereby showing that you admit a power superior to yourself.* This power is called Christ or God and if you have not this power or Christ you are not of Him. *To know God is to know ourselves, and to know ourselves is to know the difference between Science and error.* Error is of man and truth is of God, and as truth is not in the cause of disease it is not in the effect. Therefore to say we are happy when in disease is to admit we have no disease, for disease is the error and the effect. Now as opinions contain either truth or error (error not recognizes) we are affected by the effect when it comes to the light of Science and then the happiness or misery follows. This is called by the doctors disease and they treat the effect, denying the cause or letting it go as of no account. Here is the difference. I put the disease in the direction of mind and then I know what will be the effect.

Our happiness is the result of correcting our impressions when first made. Our error is the ignorance of these impressions. The opinions of the world and ignorance of ourselves are the causes of our trouble. Suppose you were afraid of some person because you feared he would like to kill you, do you think you would be any worse off to know that he was your friend and he felt unhappy to know that you had such an opinion of him? So it is in every act of our lives, knowledge of ourselves never harmed man. Disease is not in knowledge but in ignorance. For instance, *the fear of any trouble is the disease.*

Go with me back to the time of the persecution of the church and the Salem witchcraft. All the people believed in evil spirits and witches and considered it wrong to have anything to do with them. Here you see was the disease in the people's belief, and their belief was put in practice for the safety of mankind. Therefore every invention of their belief was called out to get rid of an evil that was tormenting man. Here you see that they thought the belief was one thing and the evil another, and so it is in everything. The wisdom of this world sees the mind as one thing and disease as another, and reasons by saying the pain came before I had any thought about it, and I had no mind about it. . . . *So it is with rheumatic pains, the state of mind or disease is admitted to have an existence as much as evil spirits and we are affected by our belief.* If anything disturbs our happiness we fly to someone for protection and in our trouble create a form of something in the mind to locate it in some place in the body. We suffer ourselves to be tormented to get rid of the enemy, the disease, as those who believed themselves bewitched would suffer being whipped to drive out the devils. I could name hundreds of cases where persons have called in physicians and between them have made disease an enemy irrespective of the mind and the patient has allowed himself to suffer blistering therapy almost to death to get rid of the cancer or spinal disease or some other devil supposed to exist independent of the mind. The doctors who use these means show about as much knowledge as the people in Connecticut who beat themselves to get rid of evil spirits. *It is the relic of those who think rationally that wisdom will someday eradicate from the mind all disease by explaining it on scientific principles.* Till then the knife and the lance and the pills and such things that are only introduced by a show of truth not much in advance of nailing a horse shoe over the door, or sleeping with the Bible under you to keep off the witches, must govern the people. Jesus knew that all the foregoing belief was founded in ignorance, therefore He was not afraid of these beliefs."

THE OTHER WORLD

I think I can give an explanation of Jesus' belief about another world.

At the time of the birth of Jesus the people were superstitious and ready to call miraculous any marvelous thing they could not explain. Jesus had been studying into the laws of the mind till He came to the conclusion that the priests were a set of blind guides, talking about what they knew nothing of, except as an opinion, and that they were deceiving the people by pretending to have power from another world. Jesus knew all their theories and pretenses were based on ignorance of opinion, but He could see there must be something in all the phenomena. Hearing of John's preaching He went to hear him, and then saw how the truth might be reduced to a Science. Here was His temptation; if He used this wisdom for money making business He could not but meet with the same results, it must make Him selfish. So He concluded He would risk all the sneers and opposition of the religious world and stand up and defend a Science that struck at the roots of all religious superstition and public opinion and tested all things by one living and true principle. The Old Testament being their Bible, He had to explain its meaning and show that the Writers taught this great truth, so He had to speak in parables. His wisdom being based on Science that He could prove, He commenced to put it in practice toward disease. . . . All the world's wisdom was based on an opinion, and to meet it was to spiritualize every idea. They believed in a literal heaven; to this He gave a spiritual meaning, saying His heaven was not of this world of opinions but of Science, and He would bring it down to man's understanding. This they could not understand, for their belief located His kingdom in space and attached their senses to it as a place. *But the priests had condensed these phenomena into an identity called God*, had given Him power over everything they could not understand, and robbed Him of wisdom. They created a God after their own wisdom and set Him in the heaven of their own belief. Thus the priests have placed misconstruction on every passage in the Bible which condemns superstition and taken all the wisdom to themselves; while the very Science that the Bible contains is their worst enemy.

Jesus had to establish a kingdom as the priests had done; theirs was based on opinions, His on Science, so everything that they believed was only an opinion, which His Science could tear to pieces. So He begins by saying "Seek first the kingdom of heaven;" that is, seek wisdom, then all their opinions could be explained away. Then *He says, the kingdom of heaven has come unto you and ye will not receive it, that is, the Science is here but you will not try to understand it.* In the Old Testament David called this Science wisdom and exhorted his son to seek it first of all. Jesus called it the kingdom of heaven and calls on all men to seek it. If this wisdom and the kingdom of heaven were not the same, then Jesus and David had different ideas of wisdom. Does the priest call on the people to get understanding? No, that is what he fears. The priests want them to have religion, that is, to believe in the creeds which cramp the intellect and bind burdens upon them so that they can lead them. They fear investigation, for it is death to their opinions.

NO RELIGIOUS PUT DOWNS

I am often accused of putting down religion and when I ask what is religion I am told the same old story that everyone knows, to be good and to worship God. Now all this sort of cant may do if it is not analyzed, but if you undertake to analyze it it vanishes like dew before the morning sun. Religion is what it was before Christ and I think I know what that was. The religion that Christ opposed consisted in forms and ceremonies. Now why did Jesus oppose it if belief had nothing to do with health and happiness? He said they that are well need no physician. So if a person were well it made no difference to Jesus what he believed, but he came to those that had been deceived. *Well, how did he cure them? By changing their minds, for if he could not change their minds he could not cure them.* This was the way with the young man who was rich who came to Jesus to know what he should do to be saved. Now if the young man was really in danger of being doomed to "eternal punishment," as we are taught, then all that was wanted was to believe; so if his belief changed him I ask if it changed his identity or mind? We are taught that man cannot do anything of himself to save himself, but was this the case with this young man? No, for Jesus told him what to do, to keep the commandments and these were not Jesus' but Moses' commandments. The young man said. "This have I done from my youth upward." So according to the young man's story he was a very good man and Jesus found no fault with him but said, if you will be perfect go sell all you have and follow me. Now here was a 'young man who had done everything to be saved but he would not give all that he had to the poor and follow Jesus. As absurd as this looks you cannot find anyone who will comply with it, but people get over it by saying we must give up all sinful acts. Well, let us be compassionate to that young man who went away sorrowful, for he could not understand. Nor does anyone today understand.

Now I will give my construction, and if I do not make Jesus parables more understandable I will never explain the Bible again. The Jews thought they were the chosen people of God and were the best and knew the most. So riches were wisdom and they were rich in the laws of Moses. This young man came to Jesus to ask Him what he should do to obtain this belief that Jesus taught. Jesus said, "Keep the commandments." This he had done. Well, go and give away your ideas and try to learn mine. This he could not do for he could not see into it. So he went away sorrowful. Jesus' own disciples were in the same way for they said, "we have forsaken all, what lack we more?" He then goes on to tell what they must do, but they did it not for they all forsook Him. Now if it requires such a sacrifice to go to heaven, he never found one that went, for they asked Him if these things are so how a man can be saved. . . .

My religion, like Jesus', is in my acts, not in my belief. *The sick are in their belief and not in their acts, for if it were in their acts they would be better*; for to be wise is to be good and to be good is to show your goodness by your acts. So if a man is sick he is not good and if he is not good he is not happy, and if he is not good his evil must be something else than good. His goodness is Science or Christ, his badness must be an opinion or religion. Now to be born again is to separate the true religion from the dross, and I know of no better rule than Jesus laid down when He said, "by their fruits ye shall know them." I am willing to be judged by my works, and if they bear me out I know the wisdom of this world of opinions has no right to pass judgment on me.

When I sit by a person, if I find no opinion I find no disease, but if I find a disease I find an opinion, so that the misery that is in the opinion or belief is the disease. I have to make war with the disease or opinion and as there are a great many that make their disease out of the world's religion it is my duty to change the belief to make the cure, and it is astonishing to see persons cling to their opinions as though they contained real substance, when if they knew the falsity of their belief they would laugh at their folly. Now to me it is as plain as twice two makes four. I can sum up the religion of Jesus in one simple parable and that is the parable of the child when the people were disputing about the kingdom of heaven. Jesus took up a little child from their midst and said, "of such is the kingdom of heaven." Everyone knows *it is harder to unlearn an error than to learn a truth*, so Jesus, knowing that a child was free from both, took him as a parable. So the Christian world must get rid or give away all errors and become as a little child to receive the Holy Ghost or Science. This was the new birth; therefore to enter into Christ Science or the Kingdom of Heaven was not a very easy thing. So if anyone says he is born of God or Science let him show it for many shall come saying, "I am Christ," and shall deceive many, but by their fruits ye shall know them. So you see that Jesus' religion had nothing to do with the opinions of the world.

---

*Mr. Lode has published
over 30 other books
Purchased them on his website*

TruthCenterBooks.com

or on
Amazon and/or Kindle
or
ask for them at your local bookstor*e*.

To Publish Your Own Book
contact

**Richard Dale Lode
Truth Center Publishing
213 second Street
Box 424
Sioux Rapids, Iowa 50585**
or
Info@TruthCenterBooks.com

THE JESUS BIBLE
"The Christ's Version"

The Jesus Bible combines the four Gospels into one easy to read volume while incorporating the teachings of many Christian Mystics into its paraphrasing. It brings the Bible back to Christ's original teachings, and will, I believe, one day be seen as part of a great spiritual awakening. Just as humanity evolved out of the Dark Ages into a much more rational way of looking at the world, we are once again rising to a much greater level of understanding. We are beginning to know ourselves as spiritual beings rather than just men and women.

THE HIDDEN POWER

God is manifesting as You.
You are the very power you pray to.

The creative power of God's Thought made man self-conscious and able to evolve into an individual consciousness that embraces the same spirit as Divine thought. Realizing that our spiritual self is God manifesting as us transforms our thoughts and thereby brings fullness of life and the experience of our God-Self.

Someday this book will be seen as part of a great spiritual awakening. Just as humanity evolved out of the Dark Ages into a much more rational way of looking at the world, we are now rising to a much greater level of understanding. We are beginning to know ourselves as spiritual beings rather than just men and women.

A SHORT COURSE
in Miracles

Unleash the Power.

This book is very to read, yet comprehensive.
When the lessons come together the real world is revealed.

The course is *"A Course in Miracles"* in embryo. It brings the Bible back to Christ's original teachings, and will, I believe, one day be seen as part of a great spiritual awakening. Just as humanity evolved out of the Dark Ages into a much more rational way of looking at the world, we are once again rising to a much greater level of understanding. We are beginning to know ourselves as spiritual beings rather than just men and women.

A NEW BIBLE for a NEW AGE
"The Making of a Spiritual Self"

This "New Age Bible for the 3rd Millennium" is scientifically accurate and based upon sound psychology and critical thinking. The logic presented makes it both powerful and practical for this new age of technology.

The book incorporates the knowledge of many Christian Mystics into its paraphrasing without altering the teachings of Jesus. In fact, it brings the Bible back to Christ's original teachings, and will, I believe, one day be seen as part of a great spiritual awakening. Just as humanity evolved out of the Dark Ages into a much more rational way of looking at the world, we are once again rising to a much greater level of understanding. We are beginning to know ourselves as spiritual beings rather than just men and women.

HEAL the WAY JESUS HEALED
Unleash your Power

These procedures are proven Metaphysical healings as recorded in the Quimby manuscripts.

According to Dr. Quimby disease develops from a false belief in the mind. By undermining the belief's foundation, the disease gives way. It does not matter how far the disease has progressed, its continuation depends upon a false belief for its existence. By identifying the person's belief associated with the disease you make a change in the mind; this change of mind ends the disease; and that is the cure.

I believe this book will one day be seen as part of a great spiritual awakening. Just as humanity evolved out of the Dark Ages into a much more rational way of looking at life, we are now rising to a much more rational way of looking at healing. We are beginning to understand that we are spiritual beings, able to use our minds to heal our bodies through correct thinking.

CHRIST'S GREATEST SERMONS
Unleash the Power

In this reading we will consider together a Truth Jesus taught and yet the world has not learned. The Truth is you are not your outward and visible form; this feeble self is not your real self.

Your real self is above and beyond the conception of finite mind. It is infinitely loving and filling all space. As your eyes open to this all-pervading you, true life becomes seen and is always the answer to the deepest and highest aspirations of the soul. Thank God for this spiritual self. It is this He created in His own image.

I believe this book will one day be seen as part of a great spiritual awakening. Just as humanity evolved out of the Dark Ages into a much more rational way of looking at the world, we are once again rising to a much greater level of understanding. We are beginning to know ourselves as spiritual beings rather than just men and women.

THE HIDDEN MAGIC
"at the Center"

Lode's book is a thirty-day reading on learning to attaining a sense of "wholeness" through recognizing the creator God as your real identity.

The creative power of God's Thought made man self-conscious and able to evolve into an individual consciousness that embraces the same spirit as the Divine. Realizing our-self as a manifestation of God transforms our mind and thereby brings fullness of life, not only to ourselves, but also to our family and friends.

I believe, one day this book will be seen as part of a great spiritual awakening. Just as humanity evolved out of the Dark Ages into a much more rational way of looking at the world, we are now rising to a much greater level of understanding. We are beginning to know ourselves as spiritual beings rather than just men and women.

THE JELLY FISH
THE HONEY BEE
& ME
Using Quantum Physics to attain Immortality

The field of Quantum Physics, rightly understood, can deliver you from sickness, limitations, and finally from death itself.

Of course from the standpoint of traditional thought this is a startling proposition. Yet, both the jellyfish and the honeybee have proved them to be true. The Jelly fish never dies and the honeybee has been observed growing young. Surely what a jellyfish and honeybee is capable of doing, a human being can accomplish.

I believe this book will one day be seen as part of a great awakening. Just as humanity evolved out of the Dark Ages into a much more rational way of looking at life, we are once again rising to a much greater level of understanding. We are beginning to know ourselves as eternal beings rather than just men and women.

Experiencing A COURSE In MIRACLES is my True Story

Through an email exchange Riley and Hunter examine their religious beliefs. Hunter is a Christian. Riley is a Buddhist.

During the spiritual camaraderie an in-depth discussion of "A Course in Miracles" develops. The discussion leaves them not only questioning their own beliefs but also the reality of their five senses.

I believe this book will one day be seen as part of a great spiritual awakening. Just as humanity evolved out of the Dark Ages into a much more rational way of looking at the world, we are once again rising to a much greater level of understanding. We are beginning to know ourselves as spiritual beings rather than just men and women.

Jesus, New Thought, and the Gospels

Jews and Christians consider a harmonious relationship with a separate God to be the highest relationship possible. In contrast Eastern religions have made losing themselves in a union with God the pinnacle of human evolution.

However, the true and lost teachings of Jesus transcend both. Jesus said the individual does not lose himself in a union with God, but [instead] attains a heightened sense of individual self which includes God.

This heightened sense of individual self is beyond the conception of finite mind. It is infinite and fills all space. As your eyes open to this all-pervading you, true life becomes seen, and is always the answer to the deepest and highest aspirations of the soul. Thank God for this spiritual self. It is this *"you"* He created in His own image.

This book, I believe will one day be seen as part of a great spiritual awakening. Just as humanity evolved out of the Dark Ages into a much more rational way of looking at the world, we are once again rising to a much greater level of understanding. We are beginning to know ourselves as spiritual beings rather than just men and women.

The Life Changing Secrets of
THOMAS TROWARD
Unleash your Power

Much has been written about the law of attraction, but this law is unworkable without the knowledge of another law which is much deeper and more Powerful, the *"Law of Who You Believe Yourself to be."*

In order to make the law of attraction work we must first know our real self which is above and beyond our finite mind. This self is infinite and fills all space. As our eyes open to our all-pervading self, our true life becomes known and is always the answer to the deepest and highest aspirations of the soul. Thank God for this real self. It is this He created in His own image.

I believe this book will one day be seen as part of a great awakening. Just as humanity evolved out of the Dark Ages into a much more rational way of looking at ourselves, we are once again rising to a much greater level of understanding. We are beginning to know ourselves as eternal beings rather than just men and women.

**"Experiencing"
THE HIDDEN MAGIC
"at the Center"**

Each of us lives in a universe
created by our own consciousness.

A universe "in process"
which unfolds as the result of
our inner most sense of self.

By understanding "the Hidden Magic"
at the center of our lives
we create the world we desire.

---

12 HEALING SNOW FLAKES
Unleash your Power to Heal

Through the metaphysical teachings of Jesus the Christ you are taught how to heal as He healed.

No matter what disposition of mind you have, one of these messages will strike a key-note in your consciousness.

Keep your mind open and free to receive the healing message that best fits your character.

I believe this book will one day be seen as part of a great spiritual awakening. Just as humanity evolved out of the Dark Ages into a much more rational way of looking at life, we are now rising to a much more rational way of looking at healing. We are beginning to understand that we are spiritual beings, able to use our minds to heal our bodies through correct thinking.

A COURSE in MIRACLES
in Embryo

--- --- ---

~ Unleash the Power~

The essence of
"A COURSE in MIRACLES"
is contained in this easy to read book.

Some of the ideas you may find startling,
but if you will keep reading
they will prove themselves to be true.

Nothing more is needed.

Three Godly Principles
The I am - the God in me – the individual Godhood

When Jesus said, "I AM" the way the truth and the Life he was not speaking of himself as the personal human being named Jesus. He was speaking of himself as the universal "Christ" within all of us.

When we understand the depths of meaning in the words "I AM" we will realize we are the very power we seek from God.

This book will one day be seen as part of a great spiritual awakening. Just as humanity evolved out of the Dark Ages into a much more rational way of looking at the world, we are once again rising to a much greater level of personal understanding. We are beginning to realize when we say "I am this or I am that" we are referring to our spiritual self, not just our-self as a man or a woman.

VOICES from HEAVEN

I think you know that the passing from the earth is different for almost every individual, and is entirely what each one makes of it. The birth into *real life* should be exactly like an awakening on a beautiful morning when the dawn is stealing over the land, touching everything with a purity and freshness belonging only to the first hours of the day. It is meant that we should open our eyes and see God everywhere; awakening into harmony and peace.

This book will one day be seen as part of a great spiritual awakening. Just as humanity evolved out of the Dark Ages into a much more rational way of looking at the world, we are now beginning to know ourselves as spiritual beings rather than just men and women.

Be assured that one or all of the following messages will reach you with this understanding — *You need not wait for Heaven. The whole of heaven dwells within your heart right now— and also fills all space.*

Your Solar Plexus
the Sun God
and Auto-suggestion

There is a real sun center in us, the Solar (or Sun) Plexus. This is a nerve center situated in front of the Great Arterial Trunk that carries blood from the heart to be distributed by branch arteries throughout the body. When this central Sun is in its normal condition it radiates a life energy to all parts of the body just as the sun radiates life energy to the earth.

But when our minds contain erroneous thought the Solar Plexus is put in a cramped condition which blocks this life energy from flowing to certain parts of the body. From this cause comes every disease of the human race. Therefore just one thing is responsible for ill health, erroneous thought which prevents the Sun God from blessing us with perfect health.

I believe this book will one day be seen as part of a great spiritual awakening. Just as humanity evolved out of the Dark Ages into a much more rational way of looking at life, we are now rising to a much more rational way of looking at healing. We are beginning to understand that we are spiritual beings, able to use our minds to heal our bodies through correct thinking.

A MILLIONAIRES SECRET
to financial wealth

Learn how to become a millionaire through the use of the *ONE and ONLY Biblical Principle that Guarantees Success.*

This whole book, with its Guaranteed Secret of Success, can be read in less than 20 minuetes. However, you may need to read it many times to make sure its secret keeps working for you.

A Psychotherapist analyzes
THE GOSPEL of THOMAS

These original teachings of Jesus have been analyzed, paraphrased, and written in easy to understand terms by a Psychotherapist with 40 years of experience in the helping professions.

It brings the Bible back to Christ's original teachings, and will, I believe, one day be seen as part of a great spiritual awakening. Just as humanity evolved out of the Dark Ages into a much more rational way of looking at the world, we are once again rising to a much greater level of understanding. We are beginning to know ourselves as spiritual beings rather than just men and women.

The Mystic Masters Speak

!!! What the Mystic Masters Taught !!!

The spiritual world is not lighted with lamps or candles; it is lighted by God's illumined thoughts.

It is through these thoughts that we recognize God within our own soul and ask for no other.

Let the words of the Mystic Masters illuminate your world by illuminating your mind.

WINNING

Winning contains a profound message. We are only winning in life if we are happy. We need gain nothing to be happy, we need only discover and correct all thinking that hinders happiness. With this correction happiness, with joy and peace is certain.

Learn how to win through the use of the *One and Only Principle that Guarantees Success*.

This whole book with its Guaranteed Secret of success can be read in less than 20 minutes. However, you may want to read it many times to make sure its secret keeps working for you.

The Secret of
WINNING with FAMILY

Winning with Family is the authors first children's book, appropriate for those between the age of six and sixty.

You will learn of the One and Only Principle that Guarantees Happiness within a family.

This whole book with its Guaranteed Secret of family tranquility can be read in less than 20 minutes. However, you may want to read it many times to make sure its secret keeps working for you.

About the Author

The author has over 35 years of experience in the helping professions. Before his retirement he was employed as a Psychologist by the Iowa Department of Correction, a Social Worker by the Iowa Department of Human Services, and provided Guidance Services to Iowa Public School Districts.

Since his retirement he has become the author of over 30 spiritual self-help books. The books can be found on Kindle, Amazon, and his website - truthcenterbooks.com.

He has been married over 40 years to the same woman, has 3 children and 10 grand-children. He is in excellent health, makes it a practice to fast-walk 3 miles every other day, and is confident anyone can enjoy his quality of life by reading and applying the principles he teaches in his books.

To Publish Your Own Book
Contact

Richard Dale Lode
Truth Center Publishing
213 second Street
Box 424
Sioux Rapids, Iowa 50585
or
Info@TruthCenterBooks.com